CHINESE ASTROLOGY
and
Fortune Telling

U.C. Mahajan

PUSTAK MAHAL®
Delhi • Mumbai • Patna • Hyderabad • Bengaluru

Published by

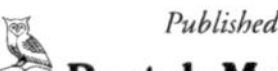

Pustak Mahal®, Delhi

J-3/16, Daryaganj, New Delhi-110002

☎ 23276539, 23272783, 23272784 • *Fax:* 011-23260518

E-mail: info@pustakmahal.com • *Website:* www.pustakmahal.com

Sales Centre

10-B, Netaji Subhash Marg, Daryaganj, New Delhi-110002

☎ 23268292, 23268293, 23279900 • *Fax:* 011-23280567

E-mail: rapidexdelhi@indiatimes.com

• Hind Pustak Bhawan

6686, Khari Baoli, Delhi-110006

☎ 23944314, 23911979

Branch Offices

Bengaluru: ☎ 22234025 • *Telefax:* 22240209

E-mail: pustak@airtelmail.in • pustak@sancharnet.in

Mumbai: ☎ 22010941

E-mail: rapidex@bom5.vsnl.net.in

Patna: ☎ 3294193 • *Telefax:* 0612-2302719

E-mail: rapidexptn@rediffmail.com

Hyderabad: *Telefax:* 040-24737290

E-mail: pustakmahalhyd@yahoo.co.in

ISBN 978-81-223-1081-8

Edition : September 2009

Printed at : Param Offsetters, Okhla, New Delhi-110020

My own observations:

I visited Bangkok in the years 2003 and 2005 to visit my children and brother, who are stationed in Bangkok. I read "The Bangkok Post" and various other articles on the "Chinese Lunar Calendar" and the "Chinese Year". Naturally, I got interested in Chinese Astrology and read relevant books on the subject including 'I-Ching' – the Book of Changes, – and occult. I was fascinated by these books. I, therefore, decided to venture into a realm hitherto unknown to one. I have attempted to write down my observations on the salient features of this branch of 'Oriental Astrology'. The people in South East Asia are enamoured of Chinese Astrology and have full faith in its predictions.

— UC Mahajan

ACKNOWLEDGEMENT

I am grateful to the following authors and publishers from whose books I have quoted and upon whose observations I have relied :–

1.	Cirlot G.E.	A dictionary of symbols; Routledge and Kegan Paul London -1981
2.	Cavendish Richard	Encyclopedia of the Unexplained; Routledge and Kegan Paul, London
3.	Anonymous	Naqshe-Rehmani (Urdu); Sheikh Barket Ali, Lahore 1925.
4.	Anonymous	Mohre-Sullemani (Urdu). Malik Din Mohd. Lahore 1927.
5.	Wilson Colin	The Occult, Random House, New York 1971
6.	Master Alfred Huang	The Numerology of I-Ching; Inner Traditions Rochester Vermount 2000
7.	Master Alfred Huang	I-Ching
8.	James Legge	The I-Ching
9.	Ajit Mukerjee	Tantra Art, Random House, New York, 1971
10.	Philip Rawson	The Art of Tantyra; Thames and Hudson, London 1971
11.	Evelyn Underhill	Mysticism; Bracken Books London 1995
12.	Richard Lannoy	The Eye of Love; Random House, NewYork, 1976
13.		Treatise on Tantra and Yantra
14.		Articles on Chinese Astrology

Contents

[Part-I]

Chinese Astrology : Zi Wei Dou Shu

[Part-II]

Chinese Book of Fortune Telling : I Ching

Correlation Between Various Streams of Astrology

Correlation between the Signs of the Zodiac in Western/Hindu/Egyptian Astrology and the Animals in Chinese Astrology:

Zodiac is a Greek word (Zodiakos – animals) which means circle of animals and is an 'imaginary belt in the heavens divided into twelve equal parts, called the Signs of the Zodiac'. Each part is named after a group of stars with some of the names bearing those of animals, such as Aries, Taurus, Gemini, Cancer, Leo, Virgo, Libra, Scorpio, Sagittarius, Capricorn, Aquarius and Pisces. Their corresponding animals or articles are ram, bull, couple (man and woman), crab, lion, virgin, scales, scorpion, archer, crocodile or goat, water carrier and fish.

Western Astrological signs and Equivalent Chinese signs:

Western

Sign	Animal	Lord
Aries	Ram	Mars
Taurus	Bull	Venus
Gemini	Couple	Mercury
Cancer	Crab	Moon
Leo	Lion	Sun
Virgo	Virgin	Mercury
Libra	Scales	Venus
Scorpio	Scorpion	Mars
Sagittarius	Bow and archer	Jupiter
Capricorn	Goat or Crocodile	Saturn
Aquarius	Water Carrier	Saturn and Uranus
Pisces	Fish	Jupiter and Neptune

Chinese

Sign	Animal	Period
Aries	Rat	March 21 – April 20
Taurus	Ox	April 21 – May 21
Gemini	Tiger	May 22 – June 21
Cancer	Cat	June 22 – July 22
Leo	Dragon	July 23 – August 21
Virgo	Snake	August 22 – September 23
Libra	Horse	September 24 – October 23
Scorpio	Sheep	October 24 – November 22
Sagittarius	Monkey	November 23 – December 22
Capricorn	Rooster	December 23 – January 20
Aquarius	Dog	January 21 – February 19
Pisces	Boar	February 20 – March 20

Western Astrological Signs and Equivalent Chinese Signs:

1. Aries (Ram, presiding lord: Mars)/Chinese (Rat, **from** March 21 – April 20):

It is said that when the Chinese animals were summoned by Lord Buddha, the Rat appeared ahead of others, i.e. it came first and appeared before the "Enlightened One". The Arians imbibe the characteristics of a Ram – head strong, rising temper, demanding their status ahead of others, stubborn, hot headed, interested in life of adventures, excitement. They are full of zeal, fearlessness, independent thinking. They do not tolerate any rivals, always claim to be first, i.e. far ahead of others. Similarly, the Rat is very subjective and always acts upon its anger. Rats nibble their way to destination and gobble up the food, hidden in the closets or even in the most secluded corners. They are sharp witted and shrewd, they know where lies their victim, i.e. the food, but when cornered they squeak and squirm, stamp their feet in anger to warn their compatriots of the dangers lurking somewhere in a corner. The Arians also force their way through sheer grit, aggressiveness, audacity of conduct and they ride rough shod over all their opponents and vow to crush them by hook or by crook. In this fight they may be hurt, but will never abandon their goal, which they aggressively pursue. Thus we find many similarities between Arians (i.e. Ram) and the people with tendencies of a Rat. Tongue lashing and vitriolic criticism is another trait of an Arian and a Rat. Temperamentally both are twins joined at the umbilical cord. Aries is the first sign of the Zodiac and Rat is the first year of Chinese Astrology. Rats are known to be aggressive, adaptable and omnivorous and are oversexed, they even compete with wild life for food. Like other animals, rats fight in defence of their territory. They challenge the intruders and generally fight to death. So is the case with Rams. They too are aggressive, impatient, violent and oversexed, full of anger and ready to fight to the end. Aries is the baby of the Zodiac and must have its way like the suckling infant. Obviously it governs the head, hence such persons are hot-headed at times. To sum up, their chief attributes are fire within, freedom of spirit, to be first among others, with a desire to lead, control and dominate, combative, hardy and sexy.

Taurus (Bull, presiding lord: Venus)/Chinese (Ox, from April 21 to May 21):

Ox is, of course, a surrogate for 'the Bull'. Both are synonymous and have the same characteristics. Bulls and oxen are known for their sturdiness, solidness. They are practical, full of patience, slow moving and faithful. They till the earth and hence belong to the earth. They must be ruled or dominated by some one, for when they are yoked, they obey the master. If left to themselves, they become furious and fight each other till one flees away or is fatally wounded. Don't we say, "Red rag to the bull." These bulls or oxen stamp their feet and snarl in a loud voice, whenever they are overpowered by a desire for matching. If the cow agrees, the bull cohabits with her. Their sex drive is fantastic. It rules over the 'Neck'. That is why the oxen and the bulls yoked around their necks are used for tilling the soil. We often call stupid people as "Bull headed" or "Bull shit". To sum up, the salient features of Taurus are: they are physically fit, passive, full of sexy desires and emotions, self centred, require some superior power to control and dominate them.

Gemini (Couple, presiding lord: Mercury)/ Chinese (Tiger, from May 22 to June 21):

Those born under this sign are full of energy, shrewd and always restless. Such persons run very fast, but soon get exhausted. They fail to keep the tempo of the initial thrust. They ultimately fail to finish first at the finishing tape. They fall on the wayside, but you must have seen the couple, i.e. bride and bridegroom dressed in their radiant best, so is the case with the magnificent 'tiger'.

Tiger! Burning bright / in the forests of night / what immortal hand or eye/ could frame thy fearful symmetry. (William Blake).

Though the simile is far fetched, yet it does convey the co-relation, between Geminians and the Tiger.

The tiger roams in the jungle and expresses its lung power. He is the master of all that he surveys in the vastness of the forest. In the sunlight, its striped reddish outer coat glistens so beautifully that even the hunters are awed by its graceful body and majestic gait. The tigers usually avoid confrontation with man. They are, in fact, solitary creatures except during the mating season. Suitors may fight a bloody battle and the winner leaves with the prized catch. The couples (Gemini) would also love to remain away from the prying eyes of the 'Peeping Toms' during honeymoon. Aren't their qualities akin to those of a tiger, hence a befitting correlation? It rules over the arms and the lungs. Geminians, like tiger, are known for their lung power, ego and pride. Both the bride and the tiger are beautiful, majestic looking but ferocious too, if not handled with love. "Handle with care" should be the motto.

Here is a limerick, warning people not to ride the tiger, they will ultimately end up in his stomach.

> *"There was a young lady of Riga,*
>
> *Who rode with a smile on a tiger,*
>
> *They returned from the ride,*
>
> *With the lady inside,*
>
> *And the smile on the face of the tiger."*

If not handled with a soft loving touch, the energy and exuberance of the Geminian and tiger are turned into cruelty.

Here are some beautiful verses regarding the ruthlessness and innocence of a tiger. What a paradox!

"A tiger comes to mind...
Innocent, ruthless,
Blood stained sleek,
It wanders through its forest
And its day, printing a track along the muddy banks,
Of sluggish streets whose names it does not know."

(Luis Borges)

What a beautiful picture of innocence and guilelessness and also of cruelty and ruthlessness. So is the case with Geminians – amiable, lovable and beautiful, but ruthless when aroused to anger and tantrums of wrath and petulance.

Cancer (Crab, presiding lord: Moon)/Chinese (Cat, from June 22 to July 22):

Co-relation between the two may seem to be exaggerated, but deeper study of the characteristics of the Crab and the Cat will bring home some similarity between them. We know there are many types of cats, the most prominent among them are street cats, outdoor cats, domestic cats and the most ferocious of all are the destructive predator cats. Cancerians, like cats, are moody, fickle in their affections, with sudden and abrupt change in temperament, i.e. from a meek feline to a ferocious one, unforgiving, and above-all vacillating in temperament and hence unreliable.

It is a known fact that dogs do not desert their master, whereas the domestic cats do not abandon their homes, even if the master leaves for another destination. Dog follows the master and cat always finds it way back home. Cancerians are known for their narcissism, i.e. self-love or self-glorification or self-praise or even self worship. There are instances of domestic cats gone mad. They are kept as pets and as rodent killers, but many a time they become extremely destructive predators. There is a Persian verse on such a ferocious trait of a cat: "When a cat becomes desperate, it in its utter desperation and wrath, takes out the eyes of a leopard even". Negative Cancerians also may go mad, like Narcissus of Greek mythology, because of excessive self love. Then there is definitely some co-relation between the two, as both of them are negative symbols of emotions of destructive self love and self esteem. Cancer governs chest, stomach and large intestines, breast is the spot where emotions throb.

Leo (Lion, presiding lord: Sun)/Chinese (Dragon, from July 23 to August 21):

There is hardly any difference between the Lion and the dragon. The lion's whose roar sends shivers down the spines of not only the animals of the jungle, but among the most dreaded hunters. It drags its prey to a lonely corner to prevent other predators from eating its kill, i.e. it does not share its prey. Lion possesses prodigious strength, it does not share its kingdom of forest with others. Leo rules one and only one single sign of the Zodiac, whereas all other planets rule over two signs. Lion thus refuses to share his domain with another predator. Being royal in their demeanor, department and habitats, they are proud, supercilious, domineering, brave, prone to flattery, majestic, impulsive but large-hearted and sluggish too. They are powerful, carnivorous, mammal with a shaggy flowing mane.

Dragon is a mythical monster with wings and claws, breathing fire as it walks or even flies to scare the enemies or intruders in his domain. Metaphorically, it refers to a fierce person who dominates others through sheer muscle power. Don't we find some identical traits between the two, i.e. the lion and dragon? Both possess personality and image which is larger than life. Dragon has an enormous appetite and his breath is fatal.

This sign governs the heart and it is the lion that is liberal majestic and large-hearted, being the king of the forest and dragon, the king of mythical world. Naturally, we have such phrases as, "lion-hearted", "The wrath of the lion is the wisdom of God" – (Blake), How true!

Here is a panegyric (Nursery rhyme) in praise of the muscular powers of the Lion:

"The lion and the unicorn,
Were fighting for the crown,
The lion beat the unicorn,
All around the town."

To sum up, lion or dragon is egoistic, brave, kingly, and royal in his demeanour, master of all that he surveys and does not tolerate any competitor.

Virgo (Virgin, presiding lord: Mercury)/Chinese (Snake, from August 22 to Sept 23):

Co-relation between the two may appear far fetched at a cursory glance, but when one goes deep into their attributes – negative or positive, one finds remarkable similarity. When confronted by an adversary, even a harmless snake puffs itself up menacingly. The poisonous ones, like cobra, eject venom into their wounded prey. How majestic and royal-like the cobra with his hood raised, but when he lashes out his tongue the on-looker trembles with fear. He is known for his venomous fangs. Virgoans are also criticised for their vituperative and lashing tongue. They are like snakes, hit back at their opponents with a venomous tongue. They want to be leaders among colleagues, may even accuse, insult and humiliate all with their scathing criticism. Like the majestic cobra, they are also beautiful – being virgins. It is a fact that snake gracefully slithers along and the Virgoans like snakes applaud themselves for their elegant gait. The snake, even when it raises its hood to sting, thinks that he is right, so is the case with Virgoans.

They are hard task masters and disciplinarians who think that they are the only persons who are right and ultimately they come to grief when they find others not responding and subscribing to their beliefs and opinions. They find their make-believe world shatter into pieces like a house of cards. That is the cause of their lashing tongues and rough language. This view has been recently expressed by modern social scientists. Virgo is a mutable sign and rules over the bowels and spleen.

Libra (Scales, presiding lord: Venus)/Chinese (Horse, from Sept 24 to Oct 23):

Venus, the presiding deity of Libra, is both the goddess of love and beauty, demon of lust and hatred too. When we praise a beautiful woman, we call her *Zauhra Jabeen* – "the resplendent face of a beautiful star". She radiates love, beauty, fragrance and is wooed and adored by man. She, is on her part, showers all comforts and abundance of luxury to the race of Adam, i.e. man. Virgil says, "Love conquers all, Let us too yield to love". Everyone is charmed and captivated by the radiant beauty of Venus, the goddess of love and beauty. Not to speak of mortals, even the gods fall a prey to her charms. But an angry woman becomes the scourge of man. She can make man's life a virtual hell, if roused to passion and anger. Congreve says, "Heaven has no rage like love to hatred turn'd nor hell a fury like a woman scorn'd". How true!

Now let us dwell up the various attributes – positive as well as negative – of a horse. Horses, like women, are graceful, elegant in their traits, emblem of fidelity and above all the only mammal which exudes love, harmony, rhythm, poise and loyalty towards the master. But if it is ill-treated and not properly handled, it goes berserk and throws the rider down to earth where he lies bruised and cries with rattling of bones brooding over his folly. Don't we say– "act in haste and repent at leisure". We thus find a great similarity between Libraas and Horses, both are obedient, graceful, paradigm of beauty and fidelity, but are also cruel and callous, if not handled with care and love. Here is a limerick for a beloved who lives lavishly on the earnings of her lover:–

"There was a young man of Montrose,

Who had pockets in none of his clothes,

When asked by his lass,

Where he carried his brass,

He said, 'Darling, I pay through the nose.'

(Arnold Bennett)

Here is a piece of some advice from the *Mahabharata*:

> *"Women bring prosperity. By cherishing women, one cherishes the goddess of prosperity. By cherishing women, you prevent youth."*

Shakespeare also advises men to woo wine and love women:

> *"She is a woman, therefore may be woo'd,*
> *She is a woman, therefore may be won,*
> *She is Lavinia, therefore may be lov'd.*

Venus (the goddess of love and beauty) is the ruling goddess of the sign Libra. Our sages have always advised us to be good and affectionate towards them, so is the case with horses. Are they not graceful, elegant, sleek, gentle and loyal! They have also to be wooed, coaxed. If maltreated, they may revolt and turn into ferocious beasts, leaving the cruel master to rue the day.

A Persian poet says, "In the beginning Allah took a rose, a lily, a dove, a serpent, a little honey, a dead sea apple and a handful of clay. When he looked at the amalgam – it was a woman".

– William Sharp

What a fantastic simile!

With all such ingredients – perfumed clay, fragrant rose and lily, sweet honey, eyes of the deer, gait of the gazelle and mesmerising elegance of the snake – woman at first felt elated but soon realised that all sweetness may ultimately prove to be her undoing. She pleaded with the Almighty that such a sweet candy as she is, the man will eat her up. God smiled and said, "Dear lady, keep your cool, don't worry! I have given you the most potent weapon in the form of a serpent in your tongue. Use it when you are in trouble and man will run for cover." Don't we have termagants and shrews or femme fatale (ladies without mercy) who pester men with their lashing tongues.

Primary emotion for Libra is Love and love resonates in their whole being. Love, therefore, is the chief motivating force for them. Libra, of course, governs kidneys and posterior along with that vital part of heart, which is concerned, with the most beautiful of all emotions called 'Love'.

Scorpio (Scorpion, presiding lord: Mars)/ Chinese (Sheep, from Oct. 24 to Nov. 22):

A cursory glance at their characteristics may mislead us and we may say that the comparison doesn't fit at all, but there are a few resemblances which may lead us to believe that Scorpios and Sheep have something in common after all.

Scorpion is the chief symbol of death and disease and destruction, it is, in fact, the butcher who takes the mortals to the slaughter house. The word "slaughter" is the key word. Don't we say – "like a sheep to slaughter". The foolish sheep follow their leader towards their death and extinction. They also fall a prey to epidemics and die in large numbers – one after the other.

Scorpios are full of intense energy, vindictive, sexy, violently passionate, with an intense desire to intimidate and dominate others. Their sex drive is phenomenon. When they fight, they fight to the finish, tearing apart their opponent. The sheep may say, "Poor me" in the clutches of a monster. The sheep runs with the herd even to its final extinction, so is the case with scorpion whose energy deals with the masses. Aren't 'herds' and 'masses' – synonymous? Scorpio rules over the vagina or penis (hence sexy), i.e. the private parts, anus and a part of small intestine. In Persian astrology this sign is called Behram – a blood thirsty soldier or butcher, carrying a blood soaked sword in one hand and the head dripping with blood in the other. "Slaughter" is therefore the right symbol for the Scorpio.

Sagittarius (Archer, presiding lord: Jupiter)/ Chinese (Monkey, from Nov. 23 to Dec. 22):

There is a remarkable similarity between the Sagittarians and the Monkey. Sagittarians are interested in spiritualism and are noble, upholder of traditions, religious minded, full of zest and zeal for a good cause, intelligent and well-read, sporty, fearless, free and frank, but full of bravado and given to bragging. Monkeys are the most intelligent primate, belonging to the same group to which man belongs. "Their mode of life on the tree has bestowed upon them a well-developed sense of sight, quick reaction and muscular co-ordination, and above all, a highly developed brain. They form well-organised social groups in which the leaders cooperate to protect the weaker sections, i.e. the female and young ones from outside attacks and dangers. They, like humans, become aggressive and pounce upon their victims, when teased and assaulted. They groom their fur, separate the hair, search for dirt, dust, and insects and remove such dirty particles. They, in fact, live harmoniously in groups, and it is this habit of theirs that makes them invaluable to outside dangers. Like monkeys, Sagittarians uphold traditions, behave in organised religion which they think to be their sacred duty. They tend to attach great importance to the traditions, which they have inherited from their ancestors. This mode of living among the people of their own clan is an attribute they have inherited from their Darwinian ancestors. The monkey personality lives with a form of reality which none dare challenge. Sagittarians too rigidly subscribe to a dogma or belief which they consider as most sacrosanct. Sagittarius is the lord of thighs.

Capricorn (Goat or Crocodile, presiding lord: Saturn)/Chinese (Rooster, from Dec. 23 to Jan. 20):

Saturn is the ruling planet of Capricorn. Capricornians write their own destiny and are the architects of their own fate. They are ruthless in the implementation of rules and regulations enunciated by them. Crocodiles live in their own burrows and are the masters of their own habitations. They do not brook any delay or interference. In fact, they are the strictest disciplinarians. They are the indisputable lords of their domains and brook no non-sense.

Take the case of a Rooster, he is the 'alarm clock' of Nature. In the early hours of the morning, it sings "doodle-doo" and continues repeating this sound till the slumbering man awakens. Here is a nursery rhyme:

"Cock a doodle doo
My dame has lost her shoe,
My master's lost his fiddling stick,
And knows not what to do."

Naturally the Roosters and the Capricorns would always prefer to control their own domains and dictate the rules for others to follow. Saturn and Capricorn are the governing lords of bones, neck and skeleton, so does the rooster control bones, teeth and skeleton.

Aquarius (Water Carrier: presiding lord: Saturn and Uranus)/Chinese (Dog, from Jan. 21 to Feb. 19):

Aquarius is another name for a water carrier or a pitcher full of water. The thirsty and parched throats and lips cry for water to quench their thirst. The Aquarian, true to his name, falls on those parched lips like the raindrops. Thus an Aquarian is a selfless good doer, honest to his job, man of integrity, humane, full of kindness, having amiable dispositions, generous to the core – in fact, lovable personality. Aquarians have some negative traits as well, i.e. they are superstitious, rebellious and 'doubting Toms', iconoclastic, out to break and shatter all out-dated and obsolete traditions, whimsical at times and unconventional too. The Dog is the greatest friend of man. It serves him well and remains loyal and faithful to him till the end. It follows the master when he changes his abode and never lets him down, in adversity even. Like an Aquarian, the dog serves all with selfless devotion. The dog is innocent and guileless, but there are also a few negative traits in it. They are both pets and predators. These domestic dogs, when they go mad and wild, are the most destructive like the iconoclastic Aquarians. A rabid dog's bite is fatal and highly contagious. Metaphorically speaking, a rabid person is "furious, violent and unreasoning." Such people are often reserved and shy in the matter of sexual intimacy. They are also great lovers when they break the barriers and walls of caution, timidity and bashfulness.

They are intelligent, a good judge of man and manners, timid but enraged when provoked. They can, of course, be easily pacified through love and tenderness.

This sign rules over the legs and ankles.

Pisces (Fish, presiding lord: Jupiter and Neptune)/ Chinese (Boar – Uncastrated male Pig, from Feb. 20 to March 20):

Boars, especially wild ones, are vicious, dangerous beasts that roam about in forests. Some species have become extinct and the environmentalists have sung a requiem for them, but the "Persistent Pigs" though acceptable and prolific have survived man's pressures better than other wildlife. Pigs are known for their slothful dirty life, they wallow in mud and are quite obnoxious looking. They are also foolishly stubborn. That is why we call an obstinate person – 'Pig headed'. Pisceans are also sarcastically called the "collective garbage can of the Universe" – an apt simile for both the Pisceans and pigs. They are hypersensitive, moody, given to frequent bouts of melancholy and depression, easily fall a prey to hopelessness, but are also sacrificing and humane. The fish is the symbol of a Piscean: slippery and fickle. The fish can only glide smoothly in warm water and downstream. If they are to swim upstream, they soon lose their steam and get exhausted and depressed. "Depression thy name is Piscean". Once they get into a mood of despondency, it becomes well nigh impossible for them to come out of it. Similarly, the boar too dangles between hope and hopelessness alternatively and once it falls into the swampy slough, it can never pull out of it. Thus we find a great similarity between the two in regard to their moments of depression and melancholy. Being "the garbage can" of the Universe, it naturally deals with feet and the lower portion of the body. This sign refers to the termination of 'Maya' or the deluge or flood, as it also stands for ocean (Neptune being its lord). It means end of journey and preparation for embarking upon the next cycle. There is a nursery rhyme about two little pigs:

"This little pig went to the market,

This little pig stayed at home,

The obstinate one that went to the market never returned."

———❖✱❖———

2

Animals in the Chinese Zodiac and their Attributes

As discussed in the preceding chapter, we have 12 Sun signs, corresponding to the Chinese 12 Lunar signs. We have given them the names of Aries (Ram), Taurus (Bull), Gemini (Twins), Cancer (Crab), Leo (Lion), Virgo (Virgin), Libra (Scales), Scorpio (Scorpion), Sagittarius (Archer), Capricorn (Crocodile or Goat), Aquarius (Water Carrier), Pisces (Fish). All these Sun signs have duration of one month each thus totalling a span of 12 months for 12 signs. In Chinese Astrology also there are 12 Lunar signs named after animals, but unlike Indian Astrological signs, they have duration of one year each. These signs follow a fixed course and one follows the other without any change and in strict rotation. These twelve are as follows:

The Rat

The Ox

The Tiger

The Cat

The Dragon

The Snake

The Horse

The Sheep

The Monkey

The Rooster

The Dog

The Pig

They are the Lords of the years indicated against each in the following pages. They again preside over man's life after a lapse of 12 years, i.e. if Rat is the animal lord governing your life at the time and year of your birth, then it will again appear in your life after 12 years. That is the case with other animal signs. The exact origin of these twelve animals is still not known. It is, however, believed that in the ancient times, the Jade king felt lonely in the Heaven and in order to while away his time, he ordered his advisors to bring before him twelve animals from the earth. The advisors sent the invitation first to rat asking him to bring the cat along with him, but the rat being afraid of the cat did not send the invitation to him at all. Then invitations were also sent to the ox, the tiger, the rabbit, the dragon, the snake, the horse, the sheep, the monkey, the rooster, the dog and the pig in that order.

The animals bowed before the king. The Rat jumped over the ox and started playing the flute. The king felt happy with his musical notes and assigned him the first place. The second position was given to Ox for his performance. The Tiger was assigned the third place in order of merit, because of bravery and courage. Thereafter, the Rabbit, the Dragon, the Snake, the Horse, the Sheep, the Monkey, the Rooster, the Dog, and the Pig were assigned 4th, 5th, 6th, 7th, 8th, 9th, 10th, 11th and 12th respectively, strictly in the above order.

As regards the Pig, there is an interesting story about his inclusion in the list of animals. As the Cat had not received the invitation initially, only eleven animals appeared before the king. In order to complete the member twelve, the advisors immediately rushed down to the Earth and brought the Pig, who was wallowing lazily in the mud. Thus the requisite quorum was completed. When the Cat came to know of the Rat's treachery, he at once rushed to the king and sought a place for himself, but the king did not oblige him, for he was quite late.

Some astrologers, however, contended that Cat did receive the king's favour and was asked to swap places with the Rabbit. Obviously they give number four position to Cat instead of Rabbit. Some astrologers, however, still believe that 'Rabbit' is the best choice.

I may point out that there are persons who are born on a date when the one sign is lapsing and the other is being born. In other words who are on the isthmus of the dying one and the rising one are in fact the luckiest / unluckiest ones, as they imbibe the characteristics (good or bad) of both the signs. For example, a man born on January 25, 1906 will have the characteristics of both the snake and the horse. For the rest, they are governed by the animal sign of their birth year. All other options are closed to them except to remain tied to their animal sign till the end. In order to know about the attributes or characteristics you inherit in your genes, first find out your <u>birth year</u> and then <u>month and date</u>. You will then be able to know about the Chinese animal year you belong to. Suppose you were born on 17th March 1930, the animal year is "The Year of the Horse".

1. The Year of the Rat:

Year	From - to
1900	31 Jan. 1900 – 19 Feb. 1901
1912	18 Feb.1912 - 6 Feb. 1913
1924	5 Feb.1924 – 25 Jan. 1925
1936	24 Jan. 1936 – 11 Feb.1937
1948	10 Feb.1948 – 29 Jan.1950
1960	28 Jan.1960 – 15 Feb.1961
1972	15 Feb.1972 – 2 Feb.1973
1984	2 Feb.1984 – 19 Feb.1985
1996	19 Feb.1996 – 6 Feb.1997
2008	6 Feb.2008 – 25 Jan.2009
2020	25 Jan.2020 – 12 Feb.2021

Chief traits of the people born in the Lunar sign of the Year of the Rat:

'Rats' are naughty, mischievous and playful. At times, they are audacious and over bold like the rat in the fable "Rat and the Lion" who had the audacity of plucking the lion's whisker. But they are opportunists and great flatterers. The rat won his freedom through flattery with a promise to pay back the favour at an opportune moment. The lion was once caught in a net. He roared and roared but to no avail. The rat heard his painful roars and at once started nibbling the ropes. Soon the lion was free and profusely thanked the rat, but the rat told him that he was returning that gesture of goodwill which he once had shown to him.

This parable also reveals one of the most fascinating traits of a Rat. He naturally gently and cautiously nibbles his way to greet fortune, fame, name and eminence. Thus, those born in the year of the Rat gradually and intelligently make their way through a great multitude of people and achieve their goal in life and attain top positions through sheer grit, patience and courage of conviction. Another characteristic of the Rat is that he is industrious, loves to live in a joint family, has great respect for elders and hoards wealth to be used in adversity.

Man must cultivate all these traits, failing which he will rue the day when he lavishly spends all and does not lay by something for the rainy day. Such un-wise and foolhardy persons may sarcastically call the Rat as miserly and close fisted, but in fact they are frugal. As regards their love for their parents and elders, let me narrate a true story about a pair of beleaguered rats who did not leave their old parents at the mercy of sailors who had decided to exterminate all of them to purge the ship of their noxious presence. Rats may be despised by us humans, who call themselves as the best of God's creation, but the Rats can teach us a lesson of regard for our parents.

'The Rat and its precious burden' —

Once, in a ship sailing from New York to Lisbon, the rats had destroyed a lot of grains and other provisions. The sailors got annoyed and decided to get rid of them. They kindled sulphur in the holes, fumigated them and sprinkled poison as well. Unable to endure the fumes, the rats started fleeing away, but most of them were killed by sailors. At last, a rat came to the deck, carrying on his back a blind old rat, probably his aged father. The sailors were moved with pity and allowed the rat and his precious burden to leave the deck. How could they kill the rat who was filled with filial affection? The Rat therefore teaches us the lesson of love and regards for our parents. The persons born in the year of the Rat are intelligent and shrewd. The rats saved the lives of Pandavas when they were kept in 'the palace of lac'. The rats made a tunnel to save themselves and it was a hint enough for the Pandavas to flee through the tunnel which was burnt to ashes later.

These persons live in groups to protect themselves from the enemies. They have learnt this lesson from The Rats who also live in herds. You may call it their 'ghetto mentality', but group life saves them from their foes. This attribute of theirs makes such persons loveable and endearing to their children, parents and relatives. Restlessness is the greatest hallmark of a rat. Such a person is always keen to make money by any means and ultimately he does succeed in his efforts. As a lover, he is known to be steadfast and firm towards his lady love and spouse. 'Fidelity thy name is rat'. So keep her in good humour, he spends a lot on her and takes pride in lavishing favours and praises on his sweetheart. Obviously, a woman likes such a husband who takes care of her needs and 'whose word is a law for him'. The Rat must marry a woman/man of the years of the the Ox or the Dragon but not of the Cat or the Horse. Cat is definitely ruled out as it is a hard fact that Cat gobbles up the Rat. The Rats often face many ups and downs in their youth and middle age but their childhood and old age are full of comforts and luxuries. They enjoy their hoarded wealth during the twilight years of their life. Such persons are good writers and authors too.

Every man has positive as well as negative traits. The Rats hit their opponents with scathing and sarcastic remarks and none can escape their vitriolic tongue-lashing. They hit back with great vigour, even after death their ghost does not permit the adversary to live in peace. Just as "Caesar dead is more powerful and vindictive than Caesar living, similarly a dead Rat spreads diseases, epidemics and death all around."

Another despicable trait of a Rat is that he is the most "selfish opportunist". Don't we know that a rat always deserts a sinking ship? He is a self seeking friend who can betray you and leave you in the lurch when you need him the most.

Ghalib has rightly remarked about such fair weather friends:

*"Ye kahan ki dosti hei ke banneyn hein dost nasehie,
Koi chara saaz hota, koi ghamgusar hota."*

"What friendship is this? Friends turned advisers nay mockers, Were there a healer, had there been a sympathiser."

2. The Year of the Ox (Bull):

Year	From - To
1901	19 Feb. 1901 – 8 Feb. 1902
1913	6 Feb 1913 – 26 Jan. 1914
1925	25 Jan. 1925 – 13 Feb. 1926
1937	11 Feb. 1937 – 30 Jan 1938
1949	29 Jan. 1949 – 17 Feb. 1950
1961	15 Feb. 1961 – 5 Feb. 1962
1973	3 Feb. 1973 – 22 Jan. 1974
1985	20 Feb. 1985 – 8 Feb 1986
1997	7 Feb. 1997 – 27 Jan. 1998
2009	26 Jan. 2009 – 13 Feb. 2010
2021	12 Feb. 2021 – 31 Jan. 2022

Chief traits of the people born in the Lunar sign of the Year of the Ox:

'Ox' is hard working, stolid, sturdy, full of patience, dependable and steadfast in its affection towards the master. He never betrays the owner and does all types of labour for him. He suffers, but does not complain. Such persons love traditions and stick to age-old customs and conventions. They never leave things mid-way, once they embark upon a work, they must complete it. In the process they may have to suffer a lot. Their motto is 'Excelsior' and 'never look back'. They are unimaginative, i.e. they lack fresh ideas. They have to be prodded and goaded to achieve their goal. They cannot therefore become masters. They always take a back seat and feel pleased in being governed and dominated like the stolid bull in life.

Although always at the beck and call of the master, they brook no 'non-sense' and if they are unnecessarily hurt or maltreated or abused, they hit back with vengeance. When angry, they stamp their feet, snort and snarl. It is a warning to all the on-lookers and wrong doers to run for cover lest they should be 'hurled about by their horns'. Such angry bulls take out the entrails of their victims who cry and writhe in pain. 'Never hurt and abuse the bull' and remember the phrase: "Red rags to the bull". Treat him well so that he may serve you till his last breath. Aren't they the best and most faithful servants? Being a stickler for conventions, the Bull is totally unromantic but once wedded, he is the 'paradigm of fidelity and love for his partner'. I remember Gabriel in Hardy's novel "Far from the madding crowd", he was totally unromantic, but in his heart of hearts loved Bathsheba, the heroine of the novel more than his life. He did not even respond to the amorous gestures of his beloved. Troy, a rake and dandy won her through his flattering gestures of love. When she was jilted by Troy, she realised that Gabriel would have proved to be a better husband. She ultimately returned to Gabriel's loving arms and lived a life of complete bliss. The Bull does not know that woman can only be won through flattery. "Vanity thy name is woman".

Ox is a faithful lover but unromantic, crude in manners and rough in his speech, but sexually he is very potent. His natural partner in love or wedlock is Rat or the Rooster – but never the Tiger who is his dreadful foe.

Symbolical Interpretation:

It is the symbol of self-denial, fidelity, chastity and self sacrifice. The Bull never complains but suffers patiently. Jering suggests that "Bull, like the He-goat, is a symbol for the father." In fact, it is a paradigm of virtuous living. Bull is sexually potent.

3. The Year of the Tiger:

Year	From - To
1902	8 Feb. 1902 – 28 Jan. 1903
1914	26 Jan. 1914 – 14 Feb. 1915
1926	13 Feb. 1926 – 2 Feb. 1927
1938	31 Jan. 1938 – 18 Feb. 1939
1950	17 Feb. 1950 – 6 Feb. 151
1962	5 Feb. 1962 – 25 Jan. 1963
1974	23 Jan. 1974 – 10 Feb. 1975
1986	9 Feb. 1986 – 28 Feb. 1987
1998	28 Jan. 1998 – 15 Feb. 1999
2010	14 Feb. 2010 – 2 Feb. 2011
2022	2 Feb. 2022 – 22 Jan. 2023

Chief traits of the people born in the Lunar sign of the Year of the Tiger:

'Tiger' is bold, agile, quick-footed, a fantastic runner for short distances, and above all large hearted and generous. He never brooks opposition, gets excited and loses his equanimity and poise, if faced with failures. He is a volcano full of energy, power, strength and fury.

Unlike a bull, he is against all customs and traditions and cares a fig for them. He rather destroys all of them.

In the process he may be hurt and badly mauled. Tiger is a born leader. He is the undisputed king and lord of the jungle. All other in habitants of the forest pay obeisance to him and always act as a second fiddle to him. Obviously, such persons are not only real leaders but also eminent sports persons, especially sprinters and short distance runners, exploring the lands and seas hitherto unknown and unheard of, inventors, experimenters and discoverers. Being generous, such persons spend money, lavishly, especially on their 'ladies'. They are generous spenders and liberal in giving bounties. He who comes begging at their doors will never go disappointed.

They may be great lovers but being emotionally unstable and always in a hurry, they fail to satisfy their partners. Wasn't Napoleon always in a hurry? He always wanted to have quick sex like a 'puffing furnace' with the live coals soon getting extinguished with Josephine. Their motto is 'Don't do everything in style, but hurry up', for they are always restless to perform everything in haste, regardless of the consequences.

The Tiger sometimes turns into a man-eater when he relishes human blood. When bruised and injured it degenerates into an anarchist or a terrorist who is always on the prowl to pounce upon his victim and quaff off his blood. Such desperadoes are out to destroy time-tested institutions and conventions without the slightest trace of remorse and regret. In the 20th century, Idi Amin the most hateful and despised dictator of Uganda, was like a predator or a man-eating tiger. He relished human blood. We have amongst ourselves both the majestic tiger and also the man-eating one. Figuratively speaking, Tiger is a fierce or energetic person, who can be a formidable foe when aroused to anger, and also a great opponent in a game, or else a great bully or a braggart and a boastful swaggerer, a person of fierce and blood-thirsty ways, or a person vigorously aggressive and highly skilled in sports or military combat. There is a proverb – "Don't arouse the tiger in his lair." Tiger can be timid like the one chained in a zoo, mortally scared of the whip of the ring master.

These are the general characteristics of a Tiger. As regards to his marriage, he can enter into wedlock with the Horse or the Dragon or the Dog but never, never with the Snake, the Ox and the Monkey, they are certainly ruled out.

Symbolical Interpretation:

It is both a symbol of anger, cruelty and darkness and conversely of power and magnificence. In China it symbolises Darkness and the New Moon. Darkness here means the darkness of the soul (The Gita – the holy book of the Hindus – calls it an abysmal state of Tamas, i.e. to cater to the baser instincts. On its higher side it refers to strength, physical valour and capacity to do well. "Yellow Tiger", solar in colour, is considered supreme by the Chinese. It, according to them, is superior to other tigers such as red tiger, black tiger, white tiger, blue tiger and the white tiger. Yellow tiger for them is located in the centre. So is the Emperor and the country, i.e. China, he rules over, is located at the 'centre of the world.'

4. The Year of the Cat:

Year	From-To
1903	29 Jan. 1903 – 15 Feb.1904
1915	14 Feb. 1915 – 3 Feb.1916
1927	2 Feb.1927 – 23 Jan.1928
1939	19 Feb.1939 – 7 Feb. 1940
1951	6 Feb.1951 – 27 Feb. 1952
1963	25 Jan. 1963 – 13 Feb.1964
1975	11 Feb. 1975 – 30 Jan. 1976
1987	29 Jan. 1987 – 16 Feb. 1988
1999	16 Feb. 1999 – 4 Feb. 2000
2011	3 Feb. 2011 – 22 Jan. 2012
2023	21 Jan. 2023 – 9 Feb. 2024

Chief traits of the people born in the Lunar sign of the Year of the Cat:

'Cat' is intelligent, shrewd, subtle, and clever and is full of graceful manners and speech. Such a person keeps away from wrangles and bickering and always talks pleasantly. His speech is music to the ears of his listeners. Like the cat, he is attached to his home, environment and surroundings. Unlike the dog that follows the master, the Cat stays at the place. Obviously Cat is the one who lives gracefully and leisurely and spends on house to lead a life of comfort and luxury. He remains away from controversies and does not want to tread on others, corns. This lends charm to his character. He does not surrender to foes but fights to the end. He may be bruised, hurt or fatally wounded but will continue to hit back. He is the one who is not easily aroused to anger non-chalantly. He keeps his cool in most adverse circumstances. He is a competent adviser, but likes to remain behind the curtain, i.e. he shuns publicity. Cat is a great and cunning diplomat and diplomats are great liars. Don't we say, "Diplomat is one who has an oily tongue and who tells lies for his own good." Never believe the Cat when he smiles and indulges in gullible talk for he may "smile and smile and yet be a villain." His graceful manners and charms are sullied by his lies. He may fool for a while but not for all times to come.

Cat is a timid but selfish person. There is a phrase "scared cat." This throws light on her cowardice and pusillanimity. Cat is also likened to a malicious or spiteful woman who makes catty remarks against others. He wins the stranger at first sight. He knows where his advantage lies. He, therefore, is full of snobbery, i.e. he behaves like a servile cur before socially superior persons and is ashamed of interacting with inferiors. But snobs and sycophants always score over their colleagues and there lies the charms of a cat. Thackeray says: "It is impossible in our condition of society not to be sometimes a snob." A clever snob, i.e. the Cat knows whom to flatter and whom to despise. He, in fact, is the greatest psychologist who knows that flattery is the "Achilles' heel" of every mortal. They are the most shrewd tale carriers. Like all snobs and sycophants, they desert their erstwhile masters and benefactors the moment they fall from grace. As regards money, a Cat has plenty of it, because of his connections with the higher ups. He knows where and when his bread is to be buttered on both the sides. Obviously he earns a lot and like a "nouveau riche" (one who has acquired wealth recently and who displays it ostentatiously), he is quite wary of spending it. He dies rich. Cat's best partner in life is a Sheep, or a Pig and the most hateful relationship is with the Dog or a Rooster and above all the Rat.

5. The Year of the Dragon:

Year	From - To
1904	16 Feb.1904 – 4 Feb.1905
1916	3 Feb.1916 – 23 Jan.1917
1928	23 Jan.1928 – 10 Feb.1929
1940	8 Feb.1940 – 27 Jan.1941
1952	27 Jan.1952 – 14 Feb. 1953
1964	13 Feb. 1964 – 1 Feb.1965
1976	31 Jan.1976 – 17 Feb.1977
1988	17 Feb.1988 – 5 Feb. 1989
2000	5 Feb. 2000 – 23 Jan.2001
2012	23 Jan.2012 – 9 Feb. 2013
2024	9 Feb. 2024 – 26 Jan.2025

In China, 'Dragon Year' is regarded as the most auspicious and exalted. The sobriquet or nickname for China is 'Dragon', as 'John Bull' is for the English. Don't we fear the dragon, when he is aroused from his slumber? The people born in the year of the Dragon are intelligent, wise, healthy, fortunate and full of courage of conviction, tenacity of purpose and are ambitious. They have full faith in their mental and physical faculties. They make a plan, take an instant decision and implement it. They are always keen to help others and to do well to them without claiming anything in return. Like Lions they are loners and love to live far away from madding crowds. That is one major reason for their stressful and depressed life. Normally they do not get aroused but once they lose their temper, it becomes difficult to pacify them. All said and done they are magnanimous and large hearted. A Dragon is indeed "lion-hearted".

They are brave, majestic in deportment and proud of their mental and physical powers. Like lion, the Dragon too roars and takes pride in his thundering voice. Having all the traits of a lion, the Dragon is a winner all the way. It is royal-like and must therefore expect loyalty of his followers. He is over bold and a great fighter, but sometimes he is fool-hardy, i.e. lacks cunningness of the snake and thus loses ground. Victory is turned into defeat, because of lack of flexibility in his character. A Dragon dabbles in art and drama, but often his bluff lets him down. He must remember that the stage of a theatre is different from the stage of life. It is his 'ego' that spells disaster for him. In many fables lions are befooled by fox, so a cunning and subtle 'fox' or man can hoodwink the egoistical dragon too.

For the Dragon, the Rat and the Monkey are the best life partners. Because of his muscle power and majestic height, he is the darling of the fair sex.

Symbolical Interpretation:

Diel suggests that the generic 'Dragon of China is the symbol of victory, domination over the wickedness and sublimation'. It is regarded as the emblem of

Imperial authority and power. That was why the ancient emperors of China used to have five-clawed dragons and their courtiers only four-clawed dragons. Frazer tells us "the Chinese whenever they wish for rains, make a huge dragon out of wood and paper and carry it in a procession. If it does not rain, they destroy the dragon." According to the Chinese, the Dragon and the Serpent symbolise "Rhythmic life". All ancient Chinese texts refer to the association of the Dragon with lightning, rain, fecundity and power of creation. It is a celestial animal full of power, strength and speed.

6. The Year of the Snake:

Year	From - To
1905	4 Feb.1905 – 25 Jan.1906
1917	23 Jan.1917 – 11 Feb.1918
1929	10 Feb.1929 – 29 Jan.1930
1941	27 Jan.1941 – 15 Feb.1942
1953	14 Feb.1953 – 3 Feb.1954
1965	2 Feb. 1965 – 21 Jan.1966
1977	18 Feb.1977 – 6 Feb.1978
1989	6 Feb.1989 – 26 Jan.1990
2001	24 Jan.2001 – 11 Feb.2002
2013	10 Feb.2013 – 30 Jan.2014
2025	29 Jan.2025 – 17 Feb.2026

'Snake' is associated with beauty, grace, elegance and captivating charms, but also with fear and terror. It is man's greatest friend for it gobbles up the Rats, but if aroused, it raises its hood and strikes with a vengeance which sends shivers down the spine. He does possess such a fascinating beauty which petrifies the man and he gazes and gazes at such a marvelous creature.

Snake is also associated with wisdom and caution. It never strikes first, but hits back aggressively and injects fatal poison in his victim. Another quality of a snake is his capacity to take instant decision and to remain firm till it is implemented in toto. 'Instant action' is a by-word for a snake.

Snakes hibernate during winters. In other words, Snakes are stingy, hoard their wealth and strength to utilise it at the opportune moment. Thus they are rich but miserly. They are bad moneylenders. They must get back their money with exorbitant interest. Can't we compare them with 'Pathans'? "It is said that one borrows money from a Pathan at his peril. If you fail to repay it, the burly Pathan crushes the borrower's body in his 'octopus-like' grip." Shylock must have his pound of flesh, in the same way Snake must get back his money or else be prepared for the worst. He will paralyse your body in his embrace. "Beware, before borrowing from such a dangerous moneylender." Though wise, placid and calm, they meander their way to their goal. In the process, they may have to ride rough shod over enemies. "Never pick quarrel with a snake, you will be a big loser, and never step over it, it will sting you to your death." Snakes are great lovers. They are known for their fidelity to each other. We have folk lore extolling the love legends of snakes. When we say marriage binds the lovers in a sacred thread that lasts for many lives, we actually refer to snakes whose love extends to many lives. In their case even death does not play the villainous role, for they meet each other in the life after death even. They are attractive and sexy. They dance to the tunes of the flute. Naturally they are inborn dancers and hence 'ladies men'. Women fall for them. "Apparels oft proclaim a man", says Shakespeare. It befits the snakes the most. Their dress, i.e. the outer skin, is resplendent and fascinating, captivating. The on-looker is petrified in his shoes. They often change their dress and come out with a more attractive one, hence they always look tidy. Doesn't Snake cast his skin? Their best partners in wedlock are Bull and the Pig. Tiger is definitely ruled out being his sworn enemy. Snakes are also associated with treacherous and hidden enemy and ungrateful friend in his negative aspect. Don't we say, "snake in the grass" or "snake in one's bosom". 'Snaky' sharing the characteristics of a snake in shyness, cunningness, treachery, perfidiousness, venom and spitefulness. These of course are the negative traits of a snake, but all snakes are not poisonous. There are non-poisonous snakes which are harmless and are killed without impunity, but the most dangerous species is that of cobra whose sting is totally fatal.

The romantic poets and disgruntled lovers often complain of the frailty of a woman's love, but the reverse is equally true. Shakespeare does not take sides and gives an unbiased opinion. He castigates woman for the fidelity when he says, "frailty thy name is woman", but in the same breath he upbraids man for his faithlessness and frequent change of heart. He says:

"Sigh no more ladies, sigh no more,
Men are deceivers ever,
One foot in sea and one on shore,
To one thing constant never."

If we have temptresses like Cleopatra among women, we too have philanderers like Casanovas among men. Snake is gentle and docile, but when provoked or hit, it retaliates with fury and vengeance.

Symbolic Interpretation:

According to Teillard, "Snake casts off its skin, hence it is the symbol of Resurrection, because of its serpentine movement and also because of its coils which strangulate other animals including man, it symbolises strength. Further, its viciousness refers to its diabolical intent and nature". In fact it can both kill and cure, hence it is the symbol of both the positive and negative aspects. It is the life force which represents birth and rebirth. Lord Shiva, around whose neck they coil, is the Lord of Death and compassion too. We often say that a snake bites its own tail. In Chinese astrology, half of the snake is dark and the other half is bright, obviously referring to the Yang-Yin symbols (Yang, the male principle is active, bright, lucid, assertive and positive, whereas Yin, the female counterpart is submissive, dark negative). Symbolically, a Snake means "Energy in its purest and nascent form". In fact, it is the emblem of dual distribution of forces and that is why it is captivating as well as repulsive.

7. The Year of the Horse:

Year	From - To
1906	25 Jan.1906 - 13 Feb.1907
1918	11 Feb.1918 - 31 Jan.1919
1930	30 Jan.1930 – 16 Feb.1931
1942	15 Feb.1942 – 5 Feb.1943
1954	3 Feb.1954 – 23 Jan.1955
1966	21 Jan.1966 – 9 Feb.1967
1978	7 Feb.1978 – 27 Jan.1979
1990	27 Jan.1990 – 14 Feb.1991
2002	12 Feb.2002 – 31 Jan.2003
2014	31 Jan.2014 – 18 Feb.2015
2026	18 Feb.2026 – 7 Feb.2027

Person born in the year of the 'Horse' is social, active and fond of company where he shines owing to his gift of the gab. His glib talk makes him the best politician and absolute person or a teacher par excellence. His amicable personality, smiling face and child-like innocence endear him to all. He does make a parade of his superficial learning, but his mannerism, eloquence and felicity of language make up the lack of depth and erudition in his discourses. He may not be shrewd and cunning, but he rises to the occasion when the circumstances so demand. He has the capacity to perform many deeds simultaneously. His motto is "Excelsior to move ahead and never to rest on his oars." He is self respecting, having faith in his own acumen and faculties.

He, of course, can handle money matters, but soon loses his concentration. He can be a lavish spender and close fisted too. He is in fact "penny wise and pound foolish". He may grudge himself a few bucks, but may spend a whole lot on others. He is an unwise investor and a foolish spender of wealth. As regards his love affairs, it can be conveniently said that "she is the Mistress of the house and he does her bidding quite cheerfully". It is she who wears the breeches and he is merely tied to her apron strings. Well, this may be considered a negation of his macho personality, but subservience to the 'Lady of the House' makes him lead a comfortable life. It is always prudent for a man to play a second fiddle to his soul-mate. Fidelity

– whether to the master or the mistress – thy name is Horse. He often dresses and behaves like a dandy to attract his lady love. Despite all these plus points, a Horse, when maltreated or abused, can spell trouble for the master. "Treat him with kid gloves, flatter him and enjoy a wonderful ride, i.e. he will serve you well." Horses are not only graceful, but also full of zest and energy. They trot, canter and gallop to impress their life partners. They are also full of oversexed drive. Hence they need partners who are equally energetic or more powerful such as Tiger or Bull or Dog. With Rat he must never enter into wedlock.

8. The Year of the Sheep:

Year	From - To
1907	13 Feb.1907 – 2 Feb.1908
1919	1 Feb.1919 – 19 Feb.1920
1931	17 Feb.1931 – 6 Feb.1932
1943	5 Feb.1943 – 25 Jan.1944
1955	24 Jan.1955 – 11 feb.1956
1967	9 Feb.1967 – 29 Jan.1968
1979	28 Jan.1979 – 15 Feb.1980
1991	15 Feb.1991 – 3 Feb.1992
2003	1 Feb.2003 – 21 Jan.2004
2015	19 Feb.2015 – 7 Feb.2016
2027	7 Feb.2027 – 27 Jan.2028

'Sheep' is shy, bashful, peace loving, well-mannered, always at the beck and call of the leader, loves good things of life, keeps himself aloof from undue criticism, hence lovable, loves stress free environments, and rises to the top on his own merit and pleasing manners. Because of their malleable or adaptable nature, they become vulnerable not only to men but predators too. Such a person takes pleasure in following the leader. He will always remain a follower and can never lead. His habit of procrastination and dilly-dallying often leads him to his doom and death. It is rightly said that "he who hesitates and dithers is lost forever". Firmness of decision is not in the marrow of his bones. They are imaginative people, hence they can be great artists. A negative aspect of such imaginative people is that they develop suicidal tendencies. They must, therefore, be taught to keep their unbridled imagination under leash. If over-emotional or over-sensitive, they behave like abnormal or sub normal human beings. Let their tremendous potential be channelled to their welfare and that of the society at large. They must select their leader judiciously. A foolish leader can throw the whole herd down the precipice into the ravine. We associate a sheep to a stupid and docile person. Being of an amicable and pliable nature, the sheep needs a life mate who may have tender feelings for him/her and the most suitable companion is the Horse or the Pig. Both the partners should be well-mannered in order to lead a happy domestic life.

In this world of predators, greedy and over-ambitious human beings, the Sheep is easily duped and falls an easy prey to their sordid machinations and conspiracies. Isn't it domesticated for its flesh, wool, fur and milk? When we say – he is like a Sheep – we mean he is a defenceless or innocent creature who is readily preyed upon and shorn.

9. The Year of the Monkey:

Year	From - To
1908	2 Feb.1908 – 22 Jan.1909
1920	20 Feb.1920 – 7 Feb.1921
1932	6 Feb.1932 – 26 Jan.1933
1944	25 Jan.1944 – 13 Feb.1945
1956	12 Feb.1956 – 30 Jan.1957
1968	29 Jan.1968 – 16 Feb.1969
1980	16 Feb.1980 – 4 Feb.1981
1992	4 Feb.1992 – 22 Jan.1993
2004	22 Jan.2004 – 8 Feb.2005
2016	8 Feb.2016 – 27 Jan.2017
2028	26 Jan.2028 – 13 Feb. 2029

'Monkey' is clever, intelligent and always on the move. He believes in 'tit for tat', i.e. he loves those who express affection towards him and reverse is equally true. Love begets love and hatred begets hatred. He is a pastmaster in mimicry and copying human beings. Isn't he our distant ancestor in the evolutionary ladder? He is always in a hurry to do his job. The Monkey mimics and imitates human beings to perfection. Consequently, he is joker par excellence. Acting is his forte. He regales the audience with his innovative jokes and tit bits. He is, therefore, welcome in all parties, full of fun and frolic. Naturally his companionship is sought by all, because he can entertain all with his jokes, mimicry and antics. He also acts in a grotesque manner. What a delightful companion he is!

Monkey has a fantastic memory. We should learn a lesson or two from him. He never forgets an injury done to him and must take his revenge even after a lapse of many days or months. He also does not forget the good done to him and pays back with gratitude and there are many instances when monkeys have saved the life of their benefactors.

Monkey may lack concentration but this drawback in his character is amply made up by his innovative faculties. He improvises at the spot, that is why he is a humorous poet as well. It is his frivolous, grotesque and meddlesome manners that often land him in a soup. He tramples on the vulnerable parts of his audience, some times intentionally and some times inadvertently, and then faces the unpleasant music. His frivolity and grotesqueness are the most vulnerable parts of his personality, but he soon rectifies the damage by virtue of his hilarious temperament. People forgive him for they soon realise that "Monkey dances around" frivolously and play his mischievous tricks and antics otherwise he is no monkey at all.

As regards love affairs, he is a philanderer, a Casanova who dangles after his ladies like a pendulum. In the process he many a time receives hell of bashing, but simply laughs it away. Rat and Monkey are the best partners in conjugal life.

When it comes to financial management and monetary transactions, there is no business like Monkey business. Not only do these mischievous creatures know how to utilise money to their best advantage, but are also perfect masters in the art of shopping for bargains. They know how to haggle for the best bargains.

Symbolical Interpretation:

It is a symbol of both the baser and finer instincts in a man. It is dangerous as well as a Good Samaritan. In Chinese Astrology, Monkey is invested with the power of granting good health, success and protection to someone who is passing through a bad patch.

10. The Year of the Rooster:

Year	From - To
1909	22 Jan.1909 – 10 Feb.1910
1921	8 Feb.1921 – 27 Jan.1922
1933	26 Jan.1933 – 14 Feb.1934
1945	13 Feb.1945 – 1 Feb.1946
1957	31 Jan.1957 – 16 Feb.1958
1969	17 Feb.1969 – 5 Feb.1970
1981	5 Feb.1981 – 24 Jan.1982
1993	23 Jan.1993 – 9 Feb.1994
2005	9 Feb.2005 – 28 Jan.2006
2017	28 Jan.2017 – 15 Feb.2018
2029	14 Feb.2029 – 2 Feb.2030

Such a person is a social animal, industrious, rich and affluent, wise, clever, and lover of entertainment, fun and frolic. He thinks of his future plans and then implements them. He is interested in social welfare and improvement of ecology and environment. He is a man of determination, firm resolve and shuns controversies. He calls a spade a spade, howsoever bitter the truth is. He is outspoken and must express even the bitterest truth.

There is a nursery rhyme "Cock-a-doodle do" which signifies that Cock is the harbinger of dawn. He has a loud voice and the whole world is his listener. He is a dandy, finely dressed with multi-coloured flowers on his coat or hat. He flaunts his costly and ostentatious attires and feathers to flirt with the fair sex. To please his female counterpart he indulges in bravado and false pretences. He struts and walks with aplomb and elegance just to show to the other sex that he is a lover par excellence and he means business. Troy in Hardy's "Far from the Madding Crowd" was a fop and a dandy and through his foppery and ostentatious exhibition of his false manners, and oily tongue, was able to win Bathsheba, the heroine of the novel, only to be discarded and jilted later on. Cock is obviously a false lover who deserts his lady love at the drop of a hat and to have his sexual desire gratified, he can go to any extent. He showers all wealth and luxuries on his sweetheart. He is a mere exhibitionist and not a true lover. The Rooster is Dame Fortune's darling child. Though a braggart, he enjoys Lady Luck's patronage. Fortune does smile upon him, though he is a boastful person.

Despite his many failings and drawbacks such as vanity, conceit, foppery, exaggerated notions about his own greatness and charms, and above all his flirtatious ways with the other sex, he has some redeeming features too. He is not spiteful and vindictive at all, i.e. he does not harbour any ill will or malice or hatred for his enemies even. There is no such word as malice or revenge in his dictionary. He believes in the policy of 'forgive and forget' or 'live and let live'. Forgiveness is the best form of revenge and that is the Rooster's motto and message to mankind. Lord Buddha also teaches the gospel of non-violence and the Rooster is a true disciple of the Buddha in matters of forgiveness and piety. His soul mate is the Ox, the Dragon or even the Snake and the Dog.

11. The Year of the Dog:

Year	From - To
1910	10 Feb.1910 – 30 Jan.1911
1922	28 Jan.1922 – 15 Feb.1923
1934	14 Feb.1934 – 4 Feb.1935
1946	2 Feb.1946 – 21 Jan.1947
1958	16 Feb.1958 – 8 Feb.1959
1970	6 Feb.1970 – 26 Jan.1971
1982	25 Jan.1982 – 12 Feb.1983
1994	10 Feb.1994 – 30 Jan.1995
2006	29 Jan.2006 – 17 Feb.2007
2018	16 Feb.2018 – 5 Feb.2019
2030	4 Feb.2030 – 24 Jan.2031

Such a person is dependable, honest, courageous, justice loving and of firm determination and resolution.

He is a man of integrity, who can be relied upon during adversity. He is always in a hurry to grab the morsel, i.e. to make a fast buck and soon becomes impatient and loses his equanimity and mental poise. Haven't you heard of a groaning or a barking dog? He soon gets excited and is aroused to anger, but his wrath is only for a short while. His peevishness soon gives way to calmness of temper.

Loyalty, justice and fair-play are greatest virtues in a dog. He is a friend in need and hence a friend indeed. Treachery and dishonesty are alien to his psyche. He expresses his inner feelings of anger against cruel and callous society through an occasional groan or a bark, but he knows that a barking dog seldom bites. A Dog firmly believes in the 'Theory of Karma' and knows that it is his destiny to remain loyal and sub-servient to the master. He, therefore, has no grouse against his dismal fate. His sole vocation in life is to do his duty regardless of the results.

Despite being an incorrigible pessimist, the Dog is a doer. It is his inborn nature to help those in distress and mitigate their sufferings through selfless acts of benevolence. This is why he is loved, patted and respected by all. Dog never let out your secrets. He has a big heart which can keep the secrets of friends embedded deep into its recesses. Have faith in the intrinsic worth of a Dog. He will never let you down. He is discreet as well as bold. Rely upon him and you will never come to grief.

A Dog is unromantic and does not believe in cooing, caressing gently and feeling the delicate body of his mate but he is a great partner in sex. Dog has his minus points as well. When he goes astray, he is contemptuously called a cur, a despicable creature to be shunned, a stigma on society and a wily snob. Don't we say – 'a dog in a manger', i.e. a wet blanket, who does not allow others to enjoy what he doesn't get? When a dog goes mad, its saliva causes rabies – a fatal disease. Beware of such sycophantic or snobbish curs. But all said and done, a sane dog is a paradigm of all lovable virtues – loyalty, honesty, justice, fair play, selfless service to all and devotion to duty. His credentials are impeccable and his loyalty to the master is unquestionable. He accompanies the master when he leaves for other lodgings but the wily Cat stays on. Don't we say, 'love me, love my dog', i.e. to accept my friend – the dog as yours. Also beware of a Dog! If you have to hide something or to lie about, it has a fantastic sniffing power. It can at once recognise an unwelcome stranger and also trace a murderer by just sniffing. "Sniffer Dog" is a terrorist's scourge and people's friend. Cultivate and patronise him as he will protect you from the lurking enemies.

Symbolic Interpretation:

Dog is the symbol of faithfulness, valour, fidelity to the master and above all an animal who never deserts its benefactor. The Chinese prefer such persons as are born in this year, as they are regarded as the emblems of faithfulness.

12. The Year of the Pig:

Year	From - To
1911	30 Jan.1911 – 18 Feb.1912
1923	16 Feb.1923 – 5 Feb.1924
1935	4 Feb.1935 – 23 Jan.1936
1947	22 Jan.1947 – 10 feb.1948
1959	8 Feb.1959 – 28 Jan.1960
1971	27 Jan.1971 – 14 Feb.1972
1983	13 Feb.1983 – 1 Feb.1984
1995	31 Jan.1995 – 18 Feb.1996
2007	18 Feb.2007 – 6 Feb.2008
2019	5 Feb.2019 – 24 Jan.2020
2031	23 Jan.2031 – 11 Feb.2032

Such a person is honest, kind hearted with a friendly disposition. He always comes to the rescue of others in adversity. He patiently suffers and never complains. He is truthful and justice loving. He never involves himself in a controversy and is a good manager of an estate though may not be its owner. He is reliable and trustworthy. He digs his heels in the mud and all the forces of the world who may join to pull him out will miserably fail. In other words, he never budges even one inch, once he is convinced of the justness of his cause.

There is a saying in Persian, *"Zamin jumbad, Naa jumbad Gul Mohammed"* which means "Earth may quake and vacillate, but never Gul Mohammed". Likewise, the Pig never abandons his cause, whatever the provocation or enticement. Hence such a person is the best troubleshooter and mediator, though he may take ample time to come to certain conclusions. Pig-headed as he is, must be tardy in his movements of body and mind. His mental faculties may be slow to comprehend things but once he assesses their importance, he sticks to his guns.

Unscrupulous people exploit his honesty, stubbornness and truthfulness. They know that he does not cheat or tell lies, they take advantage of this characteristic of his. Obviously his virtue becomes a failing in this world infested with cheats, goons and rogues. He snorts and explodes into anger when maltreated. When aroused and excited, he stamps his feet to express his resentment. That is the time to 'beware' and to keep aside from his path, otherwise he may trample over the victim. A Pig is quite sexy. What he loses in his poor mental faculties he gains in virility and sexual potency. He is fascinated by plump and comely women and lilting music, such a captivating atmosphere, coupled with good food arouse his passion. He, obviously along with his spouse, is a hospitable host. Naturally he is at his best. As regards money matters, he is frugal and saves for the rainy days. In a nutshell, Pig is a reliable and trustworthy friend and a wise man must cultivate his friendship. He will support and side with his benefactor when he is in trouble. Hats off to the Pig in this world of crooked people.

In the negative sense, Pig is a sulky, obstinate and annoying person. When a man is hungry and does not have vegetables to eat, he eats pig's flesh. Thus he is such a 'pig-headed' or 'foolish animal' that he doesn't understand the motive of a greedy and hungry man or predator.

This is the last sign of the Zodiac in Chinese Astrology. It signals the end, but also alludes to the beginning of another one. The circle continues unabated –Pig gives way to Rat – and the 'Maya' of the Zodiac continues ad-infinitum. This is the beauty of all these 'Power animals' of Chinese Astrology and various signs (Raashis) of Indian Astrology.

Marriage Agreement:

S.No.	Year of the	Best Life Partners	Enemies	Neutral
1.	Rat	Dragon, Monkey & Ox	Cat/Rabbit, Horse	All others
2.	Ox	Rat, Rooster & Snake	Tiger	All others
3.	Tiger	Horse, Dragon & Dog	Snake, Monkey, Ox	All others
4.	Cat/Rabbit	Sheep, Pig, Even Dog	Rat, Rooster, Tiger	All others
5.	Dragon	Rat, Monkey	Tiger, Dog	All others
6.	Snake	Ox, Pig, Rooster	Tiger, Monkey	All others
7.	Horse	Sheep, Dog, Ox, Tiger	Rat	All others
8.	Sheep/Goat	Cat/Rabbit, Pig, Horse, Ox, Dog	-	All others
9.	Monkey	Dragon, Rat	Tiger, Snake	All others
10.	Rooster	Ox, Snake, Dragon, Dog	Cat/Rabbit	All others
11.	Dog	Horse, Sheep, Tiger, Ox, Rooster	Monkey, Cat/Rabbit, Dragon	All others
12.	Pig	Dog, Ox, Sheep, Cat/Rabbit,Horse, Rooster, Rat	-	All others

Opinions of Chinese Astrologers on all the Animal Signs (Additional Information):

1. Rat:

Westerners may look down upon 'Rat' as a 'bottom dwelling disease pestilence carrier', but the Chinese have all praise for this animal who, according to them, constitutes the First sign of their Zodiac. It is revered for its sharp wit and 'hoarding of all values' faculty. For them, it is the symbol of good luck and wealth. Its excellent tastes, charming, disarming and funny demeanours endear him to all. It knows who is its friend and who is its foe and naturally it protects a sincere friend and teases and pesters the enemy with its antics. It is his super intelligence that makes him discriminate between a friend and a foe.

Rats know where their self-interest lies. They hoard money and are greedy too, but are many a time quite liberal and large-hearted towards their own kith and kin. We can learn a lesson of frugality and helping the people of our own clan from the Rat. For others Rat may be quick-tempered and short-tongued, but for the Chinese it is never 'boorish' and ugly mannered. Rat is a scientist par excellence. Its urge for greater knowledge, curiosity to run into unexplored corners and holes, its ability to face challenges and its yearning for storing knowledge for future use do make him a great scientist. Aren't these the attributes of a scientist?

2. Ox (Bull):

"The Bull in the China shop" (a reckless or clumsy destroyer) is a wrong proverb. For the 'Bull' in Chinese Astrology, contrary to the above observation is sturdy, solid and steadfast. Man born under this sign is dependable and a born leader. He is a methodical and tireless worker who never loses sight of his goal. Behind this calm and placid exterior, the Ox does feel hurt and humiliated if not properly tended and appreciated. The Ox is indeed a great lover, loyal house maker and reliable friend. They are 'the good guys' of the Chinese Zodiac and hence no pushovers. If you are keen to have a reliable partner, think of the Ox.

3. Tiger:

The king of jungle is authoritative, self-possessed with a magnetic charm, courageous, noble, warm-hearted and a fighter to the bitter end. He is loner too. The opponent fears him and runs for cover. The best advice to all is "Do not provoke him, if you value your life." Tiger is also susceptible to frequent emotional outbursts and that is the greatest flaw in his character. If he adopts the middle path or 'the path of moderation', the Tiger can touch new heights of power, pelf and eminence.

4. Cat or Rabbit:

I have already discussed the prominent traits of Cat, but some Chinese Astrologers assign this sign to Rabbit instead of Cat. Let us also dwell upon the various characteristics – positive and negative – of the Rabbit. Being timid, compassionate, attractive and sweet natured, the Rabbit is extremely popular among all. He is an idealist in romantic field and hence gives more than what he receives. An idealist suffers in this pragmatic world. But there is a redeeming feature, i.e. he receives all help from friends and family members whenever he is depressed and stressed. Naturally this delicate creature needs solid base and a coterie of good friends to soothe his ruffled feelings whenever he is in trouble. He soon loses his balance at the very sight of a formidable enemy. He flees from the battlefield in order to avoid a fight. The passionate Rabbit relapses into a brooding or contemplative mood. If married to the right partner, the Rabbit can make the most loyal and loving spouse. He needs a protective shield when in trouble and that is why the life partner should understand his sensitive nature and provide him all pleasures and comforts.

5. Dragon:

It is the most powerful and fortunate of all the Chinese signs. Dragon is full of energy, courage, stamina, strength with a fascinating personality. They are lucky in love and career. They are born leaders and are very rich. They do not take things lying down.

6. Snake:

Snake is diplomatic, seductive, sensual, introvert, intuitive, tight fisted, though having bag full of money, mentally and physically agile, bibliophile, or a voracious reader, jealous and possessive lover, but a loving partner demanding loyalty from the spouse, dangerous and disarmingly smart, guided more by heart than by logic. The best advice for all is "not to tread upon his toes, otherwise he will have to suffer his poisonous stings". Snakes are advised to be humble and modest. Thus they will achieve great heights of success.

7. Horse:

Horses are nicknamed as the 'nomads' of the Chinese Zodiac. Like the wandering nomads they also, need large pastures and huge open spaces where they can freely canter or gallop or run about. The Horse is in fact the power house of energy, agility, ceaseless activity and lot of curiosity to gain more and more of knowledge and even money. They yearn for freedom, love and intimacy. He is always keen to travel to 'fresh woods and new pastures'. In other words, Horse is a born traveller.

Their agility and magnetic charm endear them to the opposite sex. They are romantic and hence full of seductive charms. They are 'seducers' because of their sharp and scintillating presence, magnetic personality, elegant gait and soft but sturdy skin. They are blessed with the gift of the gab and hence they carry the day in all social gatherings. But they are impatient too and it is this flaw in their character which is exploited by their foes. Though impatience is a drawback in his character, yet it sometimes becomes a blessing too. He rides rough shod over others and gallops ahead of all competitors. They are eccentric in their behaviour and this whimsicality leads to his ruin in relationship with spouse, colleagues, and officers. They must curb their wandering propensities, impatience and the tendencies to do things by halves in order to succeed in life.

8. Sheep or Goat:

Day dreaming is in the very psyche of a Sheep. It is a creative or esoteric sign of the Chinese Zodiac and needs plenty of time to remain alone and to day-dream. The Sheep is a skilled artisan or a competent teacher or any other profession which allows a free flow of imagination. Being denizens of the realm of imagination, the Sheep are not materialistic. The Sheep, when in love, offers lavish gifts to the lover. Being artistic in temperament, the Sheep feels insecure not only in love but also in all other enterprises. They are quite emotional and they soon lose their mental equilibrium. They are indeed a 'worrying lot', but can be easily pleased with a few words of appreciation and a glance of love. Thus the spouse must know the Sheep's temperament and can easily win over him or her or lose him or her through obduracy and callousness. If well treated, the Sheep does return the favour manifold. If a Sheep is able to control his emotions, life will be a garden full of blooming roses.

9. Monkey:

Monkey is the 'buffoon' or 'the fool' of the Chinese Zodiac. 'Mimicry' or 'buffoonery' thy name is Monkey. Like Shakespeare's fools, Monkey hides wisdom under the veneer of mimicry, pranks and buffoonery. Monkey is a charming, energetic party animal. You must have seen a monkey swinging from one branch of a tree to another effortlessly, similarly a Monkey hops and jumps from one group of friends to another to the delight of all. They at once become celebrities among the people, because of their ready wit and incisively sharp mind. Their intelligence also enables them to overcome all obstacles with ease. Their flaws irritate also, viz. their tendency to show off, lack of morality and fidelity towards partner, love for self, i.e. narcissistic-like behaviour, care-free in all ventures, and escapades in others domain. He does not know what is remorse or repentance in the matter of love, He is notorious for his devil-may-care attitude, self indulgence and above all non seriousness in all relationships. The Monkey cannot exercise control over his desires and urges for alcohol, food and women. A Monkey may break other's hearts, but never his own. Like a butterfly, he flirts from one flower on to an other to suck honey and desert them later.

10. Rooster:

The Rooster has been nicknamed as the 'Strutting Peacock' of the Chinese Zodiac. They are keenly observant, as if they were blessed with eyes on the back of head. Nothing can escape their keen eye-sight and observations. Their keenness for even the minutest details and their analytical faculties make them good surgeons, lawyers and marketing or financial executives. They are not mean but are straightforward in all their dealings and expect others to reciprocate. In other words, a Rooster is an 'open book' who hides nothing under the veneer of sham and falsehood. He is guileless and truthful. He honours all his promises and commitments at a great cost to his life. This trait in his character is an open invitation to all the scoundrels and cheats to hoodwink him, but they must remember that the Rooster is always wide awake and these cheats may have to rue the day when they try to pull a fast one on him.

Rooster is a 'ladies man', a 'carpet knight' as 'Casanova'. He is always a well dressed dandy and a fop. He knows that apparels do proclaim a man, and ladies fall for such a man at first sight and they may have to repent later. They are lavish spenders on their clothes, upkeep and also on their 'women'. They can only be true lovers if they are married to the Ox or the Snake, otherwise they are likely to flirt and invite the wrath of their hens, i.e. spouses. His woman demands fidelity from him, which he ostensibly lacks.

11. Dog:

Dog is loyal, honest to the master, but is unpredictable at times. He may occasionally tell a lie just to extricate himself from a nasty situation. Despite this little flaw in his character, he is a good friend and a patient listener. His motto is, "Live right and fight against injustice." The dog is dogmatic, stubborn and at times narrow-minded and temperamental. He is trustworthy and demands unflinching trust from others. This extreme temperamental flaw proves to be his undoing sometimes.

His discerning nature makes him a great businessman. That is why he often has a tough time to find the right match who can understand his craze and acumen for business. He must, therefore, relax and control his high standards of probity, truthfulness, loyalty and passion for business and irrational fears. Only then he can lead a wholesome life.

12. Pig:

For the Westerners, Pig may be a despicable, hateful, slothful creature wallowing in mud all the time, but for the Chinese, he is the most liberal and honourable amongst all the men. Pig is well-mannered, well-behaved and nice to a fault. Sceptics may regard them as servile snobs because of their impeccable behaviour, but in fact they are gentlemen to their boots. A Pig takes pleasure in finery, rich food, rich environment and lavish love making. A Pig is a good friend who cares for all. To him true pleasure lies in helping others and making them happy, but he demands appreciation for all such gestures. His magnanimity is phenomenal and whenever his friends fight against heavy odds, it is the Pig who bears the burnt of fists and blows. If he is jilted in love, he takes his revenge with vehemence and venom. He is intelligent and always eager to gain knowledge. He also spends a lot of time in doing nothing and that is why he is sometimes dubbed as 'lazy'. The sane advice to the Pig is not to remain confined to his own small circle, but to open up to other groups. 'Global liberalisation' should be his chief mantra which will allow him to bloom and flourish.

3

Chinese Zodiac Signs and their Timings as Practised in Ancient Japan

Murasaki Shikibu (c 973-1016) wrote the first great novel in Japanese language, named 'The Tale of Genji'. She, in this masterpiece, gives a good example of the Japanese concept of time. Although Japan switched to the Gregorian Calendar of the West in 1873, yet the official calendar employed in the eleventh century was derived from China and was divided into twelve lunations (months) of twenty nine or thirty days. The resulting lunar year was approximately eleven days shorter than a solar year, which required the insertion of a thirteenth intercalary month every third year or thereabout to align calendrical year with the solar. In addition, by custom the Japanese year began slightly later than the Western, so that New Year's Day fell anywhere from January 15 to February 15. The beginning of the New Year also marked an increase in one's age, in contrast to the Western practice of reckoning age by birthdays. A child born in the twelfth month, for instance would turn two with the New Year.

In the eleventh century, both the months and the hours of the day were designated by the signs of the Chinese Zodiac. The day was divided into twelve units, each equivalent to 120 minutes, i.e. 2 hours.

S.No.	Hour	Modern Equivalent
1	Rat	11 PM to 1 AM
2	Ox	1 AM to 3 AM
3	Tiger	3 AM to 5 AM
4	Rabbit	5 AM to 7 AM
5	Dragon	7 AM to 9 AM
6	Snake	9 AM to 11 AM
7	Horse	11 AM to 1 PM
8	Sheep/Ram	1 PM to 3 PM
9	Monkey	3 PM to 5 PM
10	Rooster	5 PM to 7 PM
11	Dog	7 PM to 9 PM
12	Pig	9 PM to 11 PM

When Murasaki wanted to refer to the time in the 'Tale of Genji', she would say "Hour of the Horse", i.e. 11 AM to 1 PM or the 'Sun was high'.*

For the convenience of Indian readers, I am also giving below the time units of various planets:

1.	Sun	Sunday	8 AM to 10 AM
2	Jupiter	Thursday	6 AM to 8 AM
3	Moon	Monday	10 AM to 11 AM
4	Mars	Tuesday	11 AM to 1 PM
5	Venus	Friday	1 PM to 3 PM
6	Mercury	Wednesday	4 PM to 6 PM
7	Saturn	Saturday	Night
8	Rahu	Thursday	Evening, twilight
9	Ketu	Sunday	Two hours before Sunrise

We find an almost identical division of time in both Indian and Chinese Astrology unit, with some variation.

The Chinese have a proverb: "when Yang is the ascendant, Yin is born," which means, translated into our language, that when a man has devoted the better of his life to the ordinary, business of living, the Yin,

* *The Norton Anthology of World Master Pieces (Vol. I) expanded edition: W.W. Norton and Co.; New York – Pages 2093-94.*

or emotional side of his nature, rises to the surface and demands its rights. When such a period occurs all that which has formerly seemed important loses its significance. The will-of -the-wisp of illusion leads the man hither and thither, taking him on strange and complicated deviations from his former path in life. Ming Huang, the 'bright emperor' of the T'ang dynasty was an example of the profound truth of this theory. From the moment he saw Yang Kuei-fei bathing in the lake near his palace in the Li Mountains, he was destined to sit at her feet, learning from her the emotional mysteries of what the Chinese call Yin.

4

Four Benevolent Animals in Chinese Astrology

The Chinese regard the following four celestial animals the most benevolent and auspicious:

1. The Green Dragon:

It is 'a fabulous animal and a universal symbolic figure'. It is an 'animal par excellence'. It is the most auspicious of all the animals, which symbolises plenty, prosperity, exalted status and the best of both the worlds.

2. Turtle (Black Turtle):

For the people of South East Asia, especially Chinese, it has cosmic significance. Chochod writes that 'the primordial turtle has a shell that is rounded on the top to represent Heaven and square underneath to represent the Earth. Let us put it as under:

(a) Top of the turtle: Heaven

(b) Square bottom of the turtle: Earth.

Its slow movement may refer to natural evolution.

3. Phoenix (Crimson coloured):

It is an imaginary bird which according to ancient myths, burns itself to ashes every five hundred years and is then born again. It signifies periodic destruction and creation. In China, it is regarded as the king emperor of all birds and is the symbol of the brightness of Sun.

4. Unicorn or Tiger (White):

Unicorn is an imaginary animal that looks like a white horse with horn growing out of its fore-head. It is considered as the symbol of chastity and signifies the word of God. In China, it is called "Ch'i-lin" and is the symbol of an officer eminent in status, high ranking general, a person of noble breeding, and is honest and upright in his dealings. It gives out the sound of tinkling bells and is considered "the noblest of all animals."

Some, however, dispute it, as it has two horns instead of one. They prefer white tiger to a 'unicorn'.

Five Elements:

Chinese astrologers repose their faith in the five elements and their good or evil effect on the lives of the people. Here is a brief description of all these elements and their significance on the lives of the people:

	Wood	**Water**	**Fire**	**Metal**	**Earth**
Colour	All hues & shades of green	Blue & black	Fiery Red	Of all metals especially gold, silver or copper	Brown, muddy
Season	Spring	Winter	Summer	Autumn	Every third month of every season
Representing Objects	Plant, paper, furniture, etc.	Water fountains & aquariums	Bright light	Bells, coins, keys, jewellery, etc. ware, ceramic	Earthly object such as crystals, glass articles, etc.
Number	Three & Four	One	Nine	Six or Seven	Two, Five & Eight
Animal in Chinese Calendar	Tiger & Rabbit	Rat & Pig	Snake & Horse	Rooster or Monkey	Ox, Dragon, Sheep & Dog

*For Water — (Lao-Tse says, "Water never rests,... when flowing above, it causes rain and dew, while flowing below, it forms streams and rivers."

*For Fire — The Chinese in their Solar rites use a tablet of red jade called "chang" – the symbol of element of fire.

* Northern Hemisphere emblem of light represents 'Yang' – the male principle, and the Southern Hemisphere symbolises darkness 'Yin' – the female principle. Obviously it refers to the cultural movement starting from the North and ultimately culminating in the South.

5

Chinese Magical Squares and Occult Numbers

Here is a Chinese magical square indicating the Magic of Numbers. They regard the particular arrangement of numbers in the square as magical and full of occult significance. The sum of three numbers in any direction – vertically, diagonally or horizontally – works out to 15. It also refers to the numbers of days taken by a New Moon to reach Full Bright Moon.

4	9	2
3	5	7
8	1	6

Count the numbers in any direction, the total comes out to be 15.

I was amazed to find out the same magical squares in two famous books published in Lahore (Pakistan) in the early twentieth century, named “Mohre-Sulleimani” (Seal or key of Sulleiman, i.e. Solomon) and “Naqshe-Rahmani” (Imprint of Rehman, the divine). Here are these occult and prophylactic squares:

Fiery (Aatishi)

6	1	8
7	5	3
2	9	4

Windy (Baadi)

4	3	8
9	5	1
2	7	6

Watery (Aabi)

8	3	4
1	5	9
6	7	2

Earthy (Khhaki)

4	9	2
3	5	7
8	1	6

The above four magical squares are based on four elements, viz. Fire, Wind, Water and Earth. It is believed that they ward off all nightmares, bad dreams, misfortunes, disease, insomnia, calamities and sleeplessness, insanity, all types of fears and visit by evil spirits.

Hindu Yantras:

Let me also refer to the curative properties of the Yantras, as alluded to in the Hindu Tantra. There are many yantras, but the one similar to the Chinese magical square or the Islamic magical squares is the Occult Yantra.

Fire (Agni Tattva)

Left (Air, Vayu Tattva)

8	3	4
1	5	9
6	7	4

Right (Earth, Prithvi Tattva)

Bottom (Water, Jala Tattva)

Yantra means 'Power diagram'. Such a magical square is like a chess board where numbers are arranged in such a manner that their sum total in every direction comes to 15. 15 is therefore a magical and mystical number in all occult systems whether Hindu or Chinese or Islamic or Hebrew. In Hinduism, the chief source of all such squares is the ancient text – "The Ganita Kamudi" (1356 AD).

Hebrew Occult Numbers:

Herewith the Hebrew occult numbers which bear striking similarity to those of the Chinese or Hindu or Islamic mystical numbers.

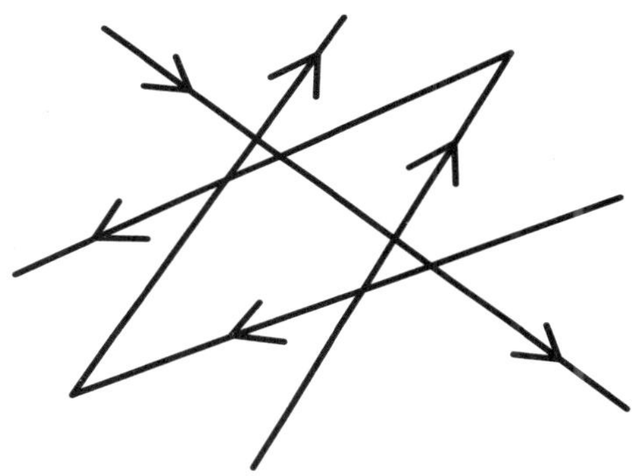

All the magical squares referred to above reveal that there is 'essential one-ness of all human thought'. These squares possessing curative properties belong to the whole mankind and should not be interpreted as the sole property of one race or tribe. "Myth", says Rank, "is the collective dream of all the people". The occult thought flows like a river unhindered by such impediments like boundaries of states and nations.

I have often wondered at this uniformity in the occult thought in Islam, Chinese, Hinduism and Hebrew. Chinese believe in five metals, e.g. Water, Fire, Earth, Metal and Wood. Human beings are born under the influence of one of these elements. Islamic occultists also believe in Aabi (water), Aatishi (fire), Baadi (wind) and Khhaki (earth). St. Francis addresses these elements as 'My little sisters the birds, Brother Sun, Sister Water, Mother Earth.

A dying Hindu ascetic chants this *mantra*:

> *"Oh Mother Earth, Father Sky, Brother Wind, Friend Light, Sweet-heart Water,*
>
> *Here take my last salutations with folded hands,*
>
> *For today, I am melting away into the Supreme."*

Let me quote an Urdu couplet:

> *"Zindagi kya hai, chand anasar ka zahoor-e-pazeer*
>
> *Maut kya hai, inhi anasar ka fannah ho jana."*
>
> *"What is life! combination of a few elements,*
>
> *What is death! destruction of them all."*

6

The Chinese Calendar

An important aspect of Feng Shui practice is to use a person's date of birth and ruling year elements to determine the suitability of directions for doors and orientation for sleeping and working. Use the calendar here to convert Western birth dates into the equivalent Chinese dates for later analysis of Kua numbers. Take note of your birth year elements, as this lets you know which elements will be auspicious for you.

Year	From	To	Element
1900	31 Jan 1900	18 Feb 1901	Metal
1901	19 Feb 1901	7 Feb 1902	Metal
1902	8 Feb 1902	28 Jan 1903	Water
1903	29 Jan 1903	15 Feb 1904	Water
1904	16 Feb 1904	3 Feb 1905	Wood
1905	4 Feb 1905	24 Jan 1906	Wood

1906	25 Jan 1906	12 Feb 1907	Fire
1907	13 Feb 1907	1 Feb 1908	Fire
1908	2 Feb 1908	21 Jan 1909	Earth
1909	22 Jan 1909	9 Feb 1910	Earth
1910	10 Feb 1910	29 Jan 1911	Metal
1911	30 Jan 1911	17 Feb 1912	Metal
1912	18 Feb 1912	5 Feb 1913	Water
1913	6 Feb 1913	25 Jan 1914	Water
1914	26 Jan 1914	13 Feb 1915	Wood
1915	14 Feb 1915	2 Feb 1916	Wood
1916	3 Feb 1916	22 Jan 1917	Fire
1917	23 Jan 1917	10 Feb 1918	Fire
1918	11 Feb 1918	31 Jan 1919	Earth
1919	1 Feb 1919	19 Feb 1920	Earth
1920	20 Feb 1920	7 Feb 1921	Metal
1921	8 Feb 1921	27 Jan 1922	Metal
1922	28 Jan 1922	15 Feb 1923	Water
1923	16 Feb 1923	4 Feb 1924	Water
1924	5 Feb 1924	24 Jan 1925	Wood
1925	25 Jan 1925	12 Feb 1926	Wood
1926	13 Feb 1926	1 Feb 1927	Fire

1927	2 Feb 1927	22 Jan 1928	Fire
1928	23 Jan 1928	9 Feb 1929	Earth
1929	10 Feb 1929	29 Jan 1930	Earth
1930	30 Jan 1930	16 Feb 1931	Metal
1931	17 Feb 1931	5 Feb 1932	Metal
1932	6 Feb 1932	25 Jan 1933	Water
1933	26 Jan 1933	13 Feb 1934	Water
1934	14 Feb 1934	3 Feb 1935	Wood
1935	4 Feb 1935	23 Jan 1936	Wood
1936	24 Jan 1936	10 Feb 1937	Fire
1937	11 Feb 1937	30 Jan 1938	Fire
1938	31 Jan 1938	18 Feb 1939	Earth
1939	19 Feb 1939	7 Feb 1940	Earth
1940	8 Feb 1940	26 Jan 1941	Metal
1941	27 Jan 1941	14 Feb 1942	Metal
1942	15 Feb 1942	4 Feb 1943	Water
1943	5 Feb 1943	24 Jan 1944	Water
1944	25 Jan 1944	12 Feb 1945	Wood
1945	13 Feb 1945	1 Feb 1946	Wood
1946	2 Feb 1946	21 Jan 1947	Fire
1947	22 Jan 1947	9 Feb 1948	Fire

1948	10 Feb 1948	28 Jan 1949	Earth
1949	29 Jan 1949	16 Feb 1950	Earth
1950	17 Feb 1950	5 Feb 1951	Metal
1951	6 Feb 1951	26 Jan 1952	Metal
1952	27 Jan 1952	13 Feb 1953	Water
1953	14 Feb 1953	2 Feb 1954	Water
1954	3 Feb 1954	23 Jan 1955	Wood
1955	24 Jan 1955	11 Feb 1956	Wood
1956	12 Feb 1956	30 Jan 1957	Fire
1957	31 Jan 1957	17 Feb 1958	Fire
1958	18 Feb 1958	7 Feb 1959	Earth
1959	8 Feb 1959	27 Jan 1960	Earth
1960	28 Jan 1960	14 Feb 1961	Metal
1961	15 Feb 1961	4 Feb 1962	Metal
1962	5 Feb 1962	24 Jan 1963	Water
1963	25 Jan 1963	12 Feb 1964	Water
1964	13 Feb 1964	1 Feb 1965	Wood
1965	2 Feb 1965	20 Jan 1966	Wood
1966	21 Jan 1966	8 Feb 1967	Fire
1967	9 Feb 1967	29 Jan 1968	Fire
1968	30 Jan 1968	16 Feb 1969	Earth

1969	17 Feb 1969	5 Feb 1970	Earth
1970	6 Feb 1970	26 Jan 1971	Metal
1971	27 Jan 1971	15 Feb 1972	Metal
1972	16 Feb 1972	2 Feb 1973	Water
1973	3 Feb 1973	22 Jan 1974	Water
1974	23 Jan 1974	10 Feb 1975	Wood
1975	11 Feb 1975	30 Jan 1976	Wood
1976	31 Jan 1976	17 Feb 1977	Fire
1977	18 Feb 1977	6 Feb 1978	Fire
1978	7 Feb 1978	27 Jan 1979	Earth
1979	28 Jan 1979	15 Feb 1980	Earth
1980	16 Feb 1980	4 Feb 1981	Metal
1981	5 Feb 1981	24 Jan 1982	Metal
1982	25 Jan 1982	12 Feb 1983	Water
1983	13 Feb 1983	1 Feb 1984	Water
1984	2 Feb 1984	19 Feb 1985	Wood
1985	20 Feb 1985	8 Feb 1986	Wood
1986	9 Feb 1986	28 Jan 1987	Fire
1987	29 Jan 1987	16 Feb 1988	Fire
1988	17 Feb 1988	5 Feb 1989	Earth
1989	6 Feb 1989	26 Jan 1990	Earth

1990	27 Jan 1990	14 Feb 1991	Metal
1991	15 Feb 1991	3 Feb 1992	Metal
1992	4 Feb 1992	22 Jan 1993	Water
1993	23 Jan 1993	9 Feb 1994	Water
1994	10 Feb 1994	30 Jan 1995	Wood
1995	31 Jan 1995	18 Feb 1996	Wood
1996	19 Feb 1996	7 Feb 1997	Fire
1997	8 Feb 1997	27 Jan 1998	Fire
1998	28 Jan 1998	15 Feb 1999	Earth
1999	16 Feb 1999	4 Feb 2000	Earth
2000	5 Feb 2000	23 Jan 2001	Metal
2001	24 Jan 2001	11 Feb 2002	Metal
2002	12 Feb 2002	31 Jan 2003	Water
2003	1 Feb 2003	21 Jan 2004	Water
2004	22 Jan 2004	8 Feb 2005	Wood
2005	9 Feb 2005	28 Jan 2006	Wood
2006	29 Jan 2006	17 Feb 2007	Fire
2007	18 Feb 2007	6 Feb 2008	Fire

[Part-II]

‘I Ching’

(Chinese Book of Fortune Telling)

1

Introduction

The 'I Ching' (pronounced as Yi King) is an ancient Chinese fortune telling game based on 8 groups of three lines and 64 groups of six lines. It is also called the "Book of Changes or Wisdom." It enunciates both philosophical treatises and method of deviation or predicting or fortune telling. It is revered and respected in all the south-east Asian countries for its philosophical wisdom. Even Taoism and Confucianism, two major and most important religions of China, were greatly influenced by "the Book of Changes." Before I dwell upon the fortune telling aspects of this immortal book, let me explain the terms "Occult" and "Synchronicity" which have great relevance to this "Book of changes" or "I Ching."

1. Occult

In simple words it means the unknown or the hidden or the mysterious which is beyond the ambit of ordinary comprehension. Our ancestors whom we often deride as primitive believed that the world was full of "unseen forces" but with the passage of time our ability to see into the life of things got dim and completely obliterated. The lust of triviality of everyday life laid thicker and thicker over our consciousness and we became virtually blind to this precious heritage of ours. It is true that visionary gleam and glory have faded into the light of common day, but still we do have occasional glimpses of our glorious hoary past.

"Dr. Faustus" of Marlowe and "Faust" of Goethe were entrapped into the vicious circle of boredom and ennui of the rational world. The former had a compact with Devil to have access to the "Unknown"; whereas the latter yearned for the "occult" to break asunder this vicious circle of everyday frivolity and rationality. It is thus the instinctive desire in every human being – whether primitive or modern – to delve into the unseen and the unreadable worlds. This yearning prompts him to look beyond this rational world and to expand inwards.

To be more explicit, man has always felt the presence of these hidden forces around him. The 'occult' thus describes his inborn faith, inherited wisdom from his ancestors to have contacts with this mysterious and hidden world. Naturally everyone is keen to know of his future and the methods adopted by astrologer or fortunetellers or soothsayers are reading of horoscopes or palmistry or interpretation through cards, dice or coins and sticks as explained in the ancient Chinese Book of changes (I-Ching). We will deal with fortune telling through sticks and coins only.

Wilson Collins in his magnum-opus "Occult", while explaining the term occult, has coined a new phrase "Faculty X" : Faculty X is "that latent power that human beings possess to reach beyond the present..... It is the power to grasp fundamental reality and it unites the two halves of man's mind - conscience and subconscious". In other words it enables the mind to grasp the reality of other times and other places. This Faculty X is the most important part of occultism and the paradox is we already possess it to a large degree, but are unconscious of possessing it and using it too.

2. Synchronicity

Prof. C.G. Jung, one of the authors of "20th Century Psycho-analysis" coined this term. In simple words Synchronicity can be defined as "occurring at the same time". Prof. Jung argued there was a conceivable relationship between two or more events not distantly related. In his own words : which are "such synchronistic phenomena occur, for instance, when an inwardly perceived event (dream, vision, or premonition) is seen to have a correspondence in external reality or of similar or identical thoughts, dreams etc., occurring at the same time at different places". But they cannot be explained in a relationship of cause and effect. He chose this term because of the simultaneous occurrence of two meaningful but not casually connected events. "Meaningful coincidences are unthinkable as pure chance."

I have referred to this phrase because Jung coined it after reading "I-Ching and the secrets of the golden flower." In simple words synchronicity means that the accidents and coincidences are somehow or other linked to the unconscious mind. He regretted that he read this great book when he was in his seventies. He cited two examples to justify the correctness of the Oracle, as expounded by "I-Ching".

Mr. Henry was an introvert who was always in repressed and suppressed mood. He was forced against his will to throw the three coins and the resultant prophecy impressed him the most. The oracle told him of his dreams, hallucinations and disturbed state of mind. The Hexagram was no.4, which stated, "Youth folly." It also warned him not to indulge in unreal fantasies and hollow dreams. He was also forbidden to consult the book second time but when he casually consulted the Book two nights later, he paid the price for his folly. He saw helmets and sorrows.

In the second example Jung tells us of the predicament of a young man with a strong mother fixation. He wanted to marry and had made the acquaintance of a seemingly suitable girl. Jung conducted the experiment with him. The text of the Hexagram read.

"The maiden is powerful one should not marry such a maiden."

2

The System of Fortune Telling

For a man who has no knowledge of Chinese language, I Ching may not held any meaning, but it is the most fascinating of all the Lunar knowledge systems. Its study will do a person lot of good.

Now let me explain the importance of "I-Ching" as a great system of divination or fortune telling. This immortal book was written by King Wen, founder of the Chou dynasty about 4000 years ago. This book, in fact started as a series of oracles. In the beginning there were 64 such oracles or hexagrams. They were later on expanded with connotations or individual lines.

Yin and Yang

The system, as enunciated by I-Ching, is based upon the two opposing principles of Yin and Yang. They are positive and negative, or light and darkness, or female and male, active or passive principles. It may be remembered that these two principles, i.e. 'Yin' and 'Yang' are not opposed to each other but are complementary and they strengthen each other. The ancient Chinese, like the ancient Hindus, believed that inter-play between these two principles is the chief cause of all events and activities in this universe.

Shiva and Shakti

In our own Tantra system, we have Shakti (the female deity) and Shiva (the male deity); one is incomplete without the other. When they unite, the whole universe flourishes and all flora and fauna propagate. Interaction between the two is the greatest desideratum for the propagation of human race. Let me also refer to Hindu notion of *Purusha* (person) and *Prakriti* (nature). Purusha is inert matter and Prakriti is the vital force that energises it into life. Let me here refer to Adi Shankaracharya's sacred rhyme to Ardhnarshiwar, i.e. the complete and inseparable union of Shiva & Shakti into one entity: - Whose feminine side smells of blooming Champaka and whose masculine side smells of camphor. The union of the male and female principles is a symbol of eternal communion and awareness of oneness through duality. 'Devibhagvata' says, "That Male (Purusha) and Myself are the same. There is no difference between Him and Me. The Purusha is what I am; I am what the Purusha is.... The one without a second, Perennial Brahman, becomes dual at the time of creation. As a single lamp becomes dual by difference of Upadhi (condition); as a single face become dual in the form of an image in a mirror as single body appears in a dual form with its shadow even. So our images are many… for the purpose of creation, the difference arises at the time of creation. At the time of final dissolution I am neither male nor female but neuter". I have purposely referred to the Tantra philosophy of Hinduism. Just as in our sacred philosophical systems male and female may outwardly signify opposing symbols, but actually they are one inseparable entity; so is the case with Chinese male and female symbols of Yang and Yin. Thus many aspects of Hindu Tantra have Chinese affinities. Even Tibetan symbol of philosophy formed by PadmaSambhava, is based on Hindu Tantra system. The chief deity in Hinduism is the female principle, called Shakti. Her very name signifies Power and she represents the primal energy of the cosmos. Her consort is Shiva, and both together constitute the cosmos. Of the two she is more dynamic and dominating, as she alone fills the Universe with her vital fluid. A Tantric saying is: *"Shiva without Shakti is a corpse. United with Shakti, Shiva is endowed with the power to create the universe; not otherwise."*

Shiva and Shakti of Hindu mythology can be equated with Yang and Yin of Chinese male and female principles. I shall be doing great injustice, if I don't refer to Taoism and Confucianism, the two most important schools of Chinese thought. The whole premise of these two philosophical concepts is based on the I-Ching as it had tremendous influence upon them.

Taoism

It is the doctrine based on the writings of a Chinese philosopher Laotse (500 BC). The followers of Taoism believe that life can be prolonged by achieving the state of bliss what they call "Hsein". In order to attain that blessed state, one has to follow a harmonious combination of dietary, gymnastic, respiratory and sexual techniques. It is believed that earth breathes in deeply during the day time; so a man must inhale deeply during the day. Sexual intercourse may be restrained, for it drains out the vital physical energy but it is not forbidden completely.

Confucianism

While discussing Confucianism, a reference to the teachings of Mencius (372-289 B C) is of utmost importance, Confucius also believed in the doctrine expounded by Mencius: "Those who follow the part of themselves that is great will become great men and those who follow the part of themselves that is small shall become small one". Both shared concern for filial piety and established rites. Both were of the opinion that “once the ruler is rectified the whole kingdom will be at peace. Confucius, who was introduced to this immortal book quite late in life often, regretted that he did not have more years to study the book thoroughly.

3

The oracles

Here is a straight unbroken line (———) and it represents 'Yang', a male principle. A broken line in the middle (— —) represents 'Yin,' a female principle.

I have already stated that there are sixty four oracles. Each of these 64 oracles is composed of these six lines, placed atop the other.

———— Yang

—— —— Yin

———— Yang

———— Yang

—— —— Yin

—— —— Yin

May I request the readers not to get confused but to study the whole system carefully? You will soon find out how 64 hexagrams (figure of six lines) are formed by the various combinations of yin and yang. Draw two lines of yin and yang side by side in the manner indicated below. Many combinations will spring up when you pair these two symbols of yin and yang. Let us start with a pair of two lines first and then add a second line and add on and on.

I. Yang interactive with Yang ⟶ (⚌) Greater Yang

II. Yin interactive with Yang ⟶ (⚎) Lesser Yang

III. Yang interactive with Yin ⟶ (⚍) Lesser Yin

IV. Yin interactive with Yin ⟶ (⚏) Greater Yin

Thus we find four combinations here; now add the third line and you will be able to get eight combinations or eight trigrams (figure of three lines).

You must have taken a sandwich where two or more buttered slices of bread are stuffed with meat or vegetables. It is said that the Fourth Earl of Sandwich was a die-hard gambler and would eat only slices of bread and meat while gambling for 24 hours. I have purposely cited this example as these lines are stuffed atop each other like a sandwich. Go on adding one line on top of another and you will find a sandwich having sixty-four layers or patterns.

I may also throw some light on the earlier interpretation of yin and yang. In the beginning these lines were meant to convey a simple answer - either 'yes' or 'no'. A 'Yang' line i.e. (-) would mean 'yes' and a Yin line (- -) would signify 'No'. As this system was found quite inadequate to predict the future of the questioner, two more combinations, as enumerated above were added.

It will not be out of place to mention here as to why the ancient Chinese preferred the use of lines to write or any other system. In pre-historic China, predictions were made by burning a cow's shoulder-blade and cracks formed on it. An identical method of divination was practised by breaking the shell of a tortoise and to the astonishment of the ancient Chinese, the back of the sacred tortoise contained eight trigrams.

The story of the discovery of these eight trigrams is quite an illuminating one. It is said that in the ancient times, 'Pao His', a mythical figure, ruled over the earth. He looked upwards to the sky and studied its bright patterns and also those of the earth, the birds and beasts and his own body.

He, then, formulated the patterns of eight trigrams to educate human beings of the mysteries of Heaven and enable them to pierce through the veil of future in order to unravel the hidden truths.

Now let us come to the point. The question arises as to why the ancient Chinese Magi, or the wise men preferred sixty-four hexagrams. To arrive at an exact answer, let us study the fundamental characteristics and names of these eight Trigrams. King Wen thought of eight basic symbols as under:

Name	Characteristic	Image	Blood Relationship
Qian, The Creative	Strong	Heaven	Father
Kun, The Receptive	Devoted, Docile	Earth	Mother
Ken, Keeping Still	Resting	Mountain	Third Son
Kan, The Abysmal	Dangerous	Water	Second Son
Chen, The Arousing	Inciting Movement	Thunder	First Son
Sun, The Gentle	Penetrating	Wind, Wood	First Daughter
Li, The Clinging	Light- Giving	Fire	Second Daughter
Tui, The Joyous	Joyful	Lake	Third Daughter

At first the above symbols may cause confusion in the mind of a reader, but when he reads between the lines he will be able to find meanings in them. When he reads of 'water' and 'lake', he feels confused as both signify the same thing; but I would advise him to read the attributes of Yang and Yin, explained at great length in the preceding pages. These symbols go in pairs of opposites and all are complementary and not opposed to each other.

Please read carefully and you will find fundamental relationship between the two pairs of opposites; such as heaven and earth, water and fire, mountain and lake, thunder and wind. Don't these pairs allude to opposite attributes such as the creative and the receptive, violent thunder and the gentle wind, the restive mountain and the joyous lake, clinging fire and the abysmal water?

Thus these sixty-four oracles are not without meaning. They convey the hidden truth of heavens. Each of the above attributes is represented by a trigram i.e. three lines and hence each of the sixty-four oracles is made up of two of the symbols.

As regards their being complementary to each other, let me quote an Urdu couplet regarding sky and earth.

"Arsh ki ye bulandian, farash ki pastion se hein.

Unka gharrur dekh kar ban gaye khaaksar hum".

(Sky's lofty heights are due to earth's humility and on seeing her maidenly pride; we have become her humble slave.)

It is true that earth is lowly placed in contrast to the loftiness of the heavens, but sky becomes meaningless without the existence of the modest and receptive earth. Though both constitute a pair of opposite symbols yet both exist for each other.

Now let us take the attributes of other contrasting complementary images :

'Thunder' is violent and tumultuous and always in rage; but the 'Wind' is gentle, mild and temperate.

The 'Mountain' is quiescent, inert and silent; whereas the 'Lake' is joyous and always in a festive or delightful mood. The 'Fire' clings and constricts but its contrary symbol 'Water' is abysmal, i.e.

bottomless chasm with fathomless depth. Thus both the pairs of opposites are essential for each other's existence. One sustains other naturally.

To elucidate my comparison further, let me quote from swami Hariharnanda's book "The World & its significance".

"There is no power (Shakti) without a support and there is no support without a power; but exists only in relation to each other. In this way Shiva is identified with his own power (Shakti) and this power (Shakti) is himself (Shiva). From this point of view, it can be said that Yoni (vagina) is Lingam (phallus) and Lingam is Yoni.

To make it more explicit 'Yang' *(Lingam)* and 'Yin' *(Yoni)* exist for each other and one is nothing without the other.

Lao Tzu (C 551-579 BC) says in chapter II of Tao-Te-Ching:

> *"Being and not being create each other;*
> *Difficult and ease support each other;*
> *Long and short define each other;*
> *High and low depend on each other;*
> *Before and after follow each other".*

Thus these pairs of opposites are not at variance but complement each other. Hindu Tantric system also vouchsafes for this polarity when Devi Bhagvata sings, *"The Male (Purusha) and Myself are the same. There is no difference between Him and Me"*.

For the Chinese, Sky is Qian (the father) and earth is Kun (the mother). Hindus also believe that sky is indeed our father and the earth is our mother.

What a striking similarity in the occult wisdom of two ancient cultures of the Earth.

Aleister Crowley (1875-1947) studied Tantra and practised sexual techniques of Tantric Yoga. He was later initiated into the inner working of I-Ching – the ancient magic system of China. In his " The book of the Laws", he refers to the fundamental formula of 'Love under Will' – which needs the passionate union of opposites. He infact interpreted the "Cosmic Union" in sexual connotations when the whole being of the individual, both male and female, is aflame with the ecstasy of the blessed union of the two opposite but complementary forces–Yang and Yin.

4

Interpreting Oracle – Yarrow Sticks

As it is, sacred book, the questioner and the astrologer must regard it with reverence and show full faith in its sanctity. Like other Holy Books, it should be wrapped in a silk cloth and must not be touched with soiled and dirty hands while opening the pages of this great book. Both the questioner and the astrologer must first take a bath, clean the whole body, especially the hands and feet, with pure and fresh water. The book must be kept on a table covered with same clean silk cloth, and the questioner must face southwards. The questioner must pay his obeisance to the book three times, i.e. he must bow and kneel before the book three times. While kneeling, he should burn the incense and pass on the bundle of sticks contained in a receptacle three times through the smoke created by incense sticks. He should move them in a clockwise fashion. But remember it should be done 'three times', which is a sacred number.

Here, I would like to refer to the custom of Aarti (prayer) to the gods among the Hindus. The *Thali* i.e. the receptacle containing the incense sticks is moved in clockwise circles thrice before the deity and the devotees chant the sacred mantras, touch the incense smoke with their hands in all reverence. They then pass it on their faces and eyes and pray for their welfare. Similarity between the Chinese ancient customs and those of the devout Hindus is quite striking and remarkable. The reason for this is not too far to seek. Our ancestors used to visit each other's countries and this interaction between the two nations led to the observance of many identical rites and rituals. The westerners may feel astonished at such strange and weird rituals but for the Hindus it is not something strange and uncanny.

Stick Oracle

After having observed all the sacred rituals, the following cumbersome and complex system is adopted:

1. The questioner holds the sticks in his right hand and divide them into two randomly selected piles – one to his right and one to his left.

2. Then the questioner consulting the Oracle picks up a stick from the right hand pile with his right hand and holds it between the last two fingers,

i.e. between the ring finger and the little finger of his left hand.

3. Now he turns his attention to the left hand pile of sticks. He takes away four sticks at a time and places them in a heap to the left until there remain just a few sticks, preferably four, to the minimum in that pile.

4. He places the remaining ones between the 3rd and 4th finger of his left hand.

5. Now he is asked to follow meticulously the same process as prescribed in No.3 above, but now he must use the right hand pile instead of the left hand heap. Then he should add the discarded sticks to the same heap containing the other discarded sticks.

6. Finally he should put the remaining sticks in his middle and index finger of left hand.

Now the process is complete. The questioner now has a total number of 5 or 9 sticks in his left hand i.e.(1+1+3 = 5, 1+3+1 = 5, 1+2+2 = 5, or 1+4+4 =9) probably these are the only combinations one can work out. He then keeps these sticks aside, but he must do it very carefully.

The above step is only the beginning of the process of divination. In the next phase, he takes the heap of the discarded sticks and repeats the above referred to process again. This time the most possible combination will be a total of 4 or 8, i.e. (1+1+2 =4; 1+2+1 =4, 1+4+3 =8, 1+3+4 =8). He again puts them aside carefully.

Now about the 3rd step to be taken by the questioner. This is the final step of the whole operation. He again performs the same operation with the left out sticks. This time also he possibly finds a combination of 4 or 8 sticks.

Finally the questioner, after repeating the process three times as stated above, possesses a certain number of sticks in his left hand. There are most probably eight combinations of numbers in the three chosen heaps of sticks. The one that is finally arrived at represents the last (bottom) line of the hexagram. In order to find out the final solution, the whole process has to be repeated again to arrive at the other lines of the hexagram.

This process is quite tedious, cumbersome, complex, time consuming, brain rattling. Only a questioner with an abundance of patience and an expert soothsayer can follow this process. In the end the answer may be ambiguous. It needs specialised training to arrive at the exact conclusion or answer. The answers are as vague as those contained in the quatrains of Nostradamus. Every one is free to interpret it according to his own knowledge of the Book.

5

Interpreting Oracle – Three Coins

There are two methods of consulting the Oracle– either by means of Yarrow Sticks or by throwing down Three Coins. The fist method, as already discussed, is quite time, consuming and complex. It is therefore advisable to ignore this process. The Coin Oracle is simple, easy to follow and does not take long time.

Coin Oracle: Take three coins, especially the old Chinese coins which carry an inscription on one side and are blank on other side. The inscribed side is valued at 2; whereas the blank side is valued at 3. In case old Chinese coins are not readily available, the modern ones with Head and Tail can be used. It is for the priest to decide about the value. It is his discretion to give the higher value to any side if he likes. For instance, he assigns the value of 3 to Heads; naturally the Tails will carry the value of 2. The questioner is asked to throw three coins. If there is a pre-dominance of Head (three or two coins), a Yang line (-) is created. If there is preponderance of Tails, a 'Yin' line (—) is formed. When this is repeated six times, a Hexagram is formed. Then consult the 'I-Ching' for the required answer.

Let me elaborate it further. For instance, we assign the value of 3 to Heads and the value of 2 to Tails. Every time the questioner throws the coins, he will get a total combination of 6, 7, 8 or 9. The Chinese call them 'Ritual Numbers'. The preponderance of Heads will mean 'Yang (-)' and preponderance of Tails will mean 'Yin (—)'. This operation as discussed should be performed six times in order to form a Hexagram. Then consult the book 'I Ching' for that Hexagram.

Let me clear the mist further, as 'I-Ching' propounds a complicated system which needs a thorough study of the book. As explained earlier, this 'Book of Wisdom' refers to symbols only and one who understands these symbols has the key which will unravel the secrets hidden in this great Chinese classic.

Before embarking upon the interpretation of these symbols and hexagrams, let me explain the term 'Gua' meaning 'Hanging up' in Chinese language. Confucius says: "In I, there is 'Tai-Chi', which produces two primary energies, which subsequently generates four primary symbols and these four primary symbols produce eight 'Gua'."

Tai-Chi

It refers to the Supreme Ultimate. According to the ancient wise men of China, there was nothing, i.e. complete void, before the creation. This is called 'Tai-Chi'.

For the Hindus, there is nothing new in it. They are all familiar with this oft repeated assertion in the Vedas and the Gita, that there existed a complete void in the Universe before creation. Here is an extract from *The Rig Veda* (translated from Sanskrit by Muir).

Creation

"Nor aught nor naught existed then, not the aerial space, nor heaven's bright roof;

Above, what covered all? Where rested all! Was it water, the profound abyss?

Death was not then; nor immortality. There was no difference of day and night,

That one breathed heartless of life and there was nothing other than it.

In the beginning there was darkness in darkness unfolded. All was undistinguishable water.

That one that lay in the empty space wrapped in nothingness was developed by the power of heat."

I have intentionally referred to the Vedas to highlight the harmony and the fruitful interaction that existed between India and China of the Yore. There is complete unanimity between the philosophies of the ancient nations.

Two Primary Energies

Now let me explain what 'I-Ching' meant by two primary energies. The ancient seers propounded the two opposing but complementary energies of Yang (-) and Yin (—). I have already discussed them in detail in the previous pages and have co-related them with Hindu tantric sacred symbols of Shiva and Shakti.

Four Primary Symbols:

Obviously when Yang and Yin interacted between themselves, four combinations were produced by their interaction:

(a) Yang (——) and Yang (——) ⟶ ═══

(b) Yin (— —) and Yang (——) ⟶ ══

(c) Yang (——) and Yin (— —) ⟶ ══

(d) Yin (— —) and Yin (— —) ⟶ ══

Eight Primary Symbols or Gua:

With the process of such an interaction continuing unabated eight possible combinations were generated:

(a) Yang (——) interacting with greater Yang (⚌) → ☰

(b) Yin (— —) interacting with greater Yang (⚌) → ☱

(c) Yang (——) interacting with lesser Yin (⚍) → ☲

(d) Yin (——) interacting with lesser Yin (⚍) → ☳

(e) Yang (— —) interacting with lesser Yang (⚎) → ☴

(f) Yin (— —) interacting with lesser Yang (⚎) → ☵

(g) Yang (——) interacting with greater Yin (⚏) → ☶

(h) Yin (— —) interacting with greater Yin (⚏) → ☷

Let me clear the haze of ambiguity, if there is any, in the mind of readers by way of following symbols and let us repeat the above process still further and let us see what we get out of this interaction.

I. Place Yang (——) over greater Yang (⚌) → ☰ Qian i.e. Heaven

II. Place Yin (— —) over greater Yang (⚌) → ☱ Tui i.e. Lake

III. Place Yang (——) over lesser Yin (⚍) → ☲ Li i.e. Fire

IV. Place Yin (——) over lesser Yin (⚍) → ☳ Zhen (Chen) i.e. Thunder

V. Place Yang (— —) over lesser Yang (⚎) → ☴ Xun (Sun) i.e. Wind

VI. Place Yin (— —) over lesser Yang (⚎) → ☵ Kan i.e. Water

VII. Place yang (——) over greater Yin (⚏) → ☶ Gen (Ken) i.e. Mountain

VIII. Place Yin (— —) over greater Yin (⚏) → ☷ Kun i.e. Earth

(a) We find that Heaven and Lake are generated by the same source, i.e. Greater Yang.

(b) Fire and Thunder are produced by Lesser Yin (same source).

(c) Wind and Water are generated by Lesser Yang (same source).

(d) Mountain and Earth come from Greater Yin (same source)

Let us, for clarity sake, arrange these eight symbols in a horizontal and circular style:

Horizontal Position

☷	☶	☵	☴	☳	☲	☱	☰
8	7	6	5	4	3	2	1
Earth	Mountain	Water	Wind	Thunder	Fire	Lake	Heaven

Circular Position

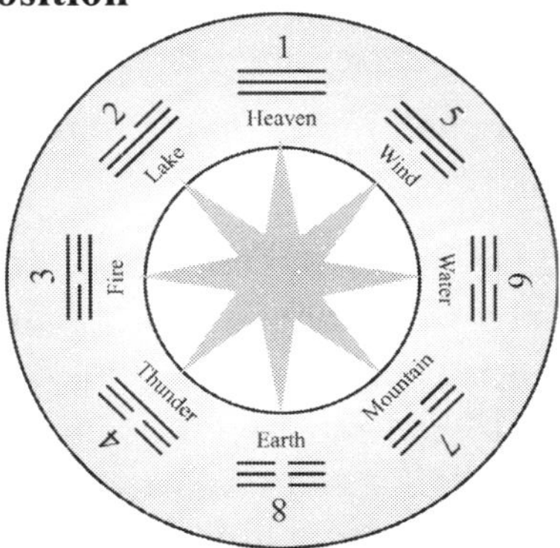

I have already explained their contrasting but complementary attributes in previous pages. This indeed is the fundamental principle of Tai-Chi (State of Nothing).

6

Significance of Number '9'

All mathematicians, numerologists and philosophers attach great importance to the numbers. They believe that these numbers are not lifeless and inanimate, but they are throbbing with life and have a living soul in them. Thus they play a significant role in our life and a specialist can predict man's future through the interplay of numbers.

"All things have form, and all forms can be defined by number," so says Pythagoras. From I-Ching to Pythagoras and Cheiro – all have concluded that numbers do play the most significant role in man's life. Should we call these numbers as 'Numbers of Destiny'? These numbers indicate one's journey on the highway of life from birth to death. The Chinese believe in the dictum: 'Predestined number is hard to escape from'.

Now let us refer to Number 'Nine' as envisaged in 'I-Ching'. In the previous chapter, we tried the horizontal and circular positions. You will find that Heaven represents '1' and its opposing symbol, i.e. the Earth represents '8'. Similarly Lake, Fire, Thunder represent 2, 3 and 4 respectively and their opposing but complementary numbers are 7, 6 and 5 respectively. Let us add them in the manner indicated below:

1. Heaven + Earth = 1+8 = 9
2. Lake + Mountain = 2+7 = 9
3. Fire + Water = 3+6 = 9
4. Thunder + Wind = 4+5 = 9

Thus we find four pairs each having number 9. Now multiply these four pairs and it will be 4x9 = 36, i.e. 3+6 = 9.

Further let us also study the lines → one complete line (–) for Yang → two lines broken in the middle (–) for Yin. Surprisingly we find the sacred number 9 in each opposing symbol.

I. Heaven ☰ + Earth ☷ → 3 + 6 = 9

II. Lake ☱ + Mountain ☶ → 5 + 4 = 9

III. Fire ☲ + Water ☵ → 4 + 5 = 9

IV. Thunder ☳ + Wind ☴ → 5 + 4 = 9

Multiply 4x9, we arrive at the double digit of 36, i.e. 3+6 = 9. Now let us understand the importance of the sacred number '9'.

The Sacred Number

According to all the ancient as well as modern sages, number 9 is the most sanctified number. Colin Wilson, in his famous book 'The Occult', writes : *"Nine is the royal number, associated with a high degree of creativity (The Nine Muses) and spiritual achievements. Nines are visionaries and poets at their best".*

Cheiro, while explaining the importance of number 9 in the 'Scheme of things', refers to the mysterious text in 'Revelation' Chapter XIII, Verse No.18: *"Here is wisdom. Let him that had understanding count the number of the beast, for it is the number of man and his number is 666".*

Let us add all these digits and you will find No.18 i.e. 1+8 = 9 (the heavenly number).

This number 9 represents the nine planets of the solar system. With the discovery of Uranus and Neptune, the number has gone up to 9 instead of earlier number 7. Uranus was discovered in 18th century, i.e. 1+8 = 9 and Neptune was discovered in year 1845, i.e. 1+8+4+5 = 18, i.e. 1+8 = 9.

All our calculations are built up on the pyramid of 9. Beyond this we can not go except to repeat the numbers 1 to 9 (1+2+3+4+5+6+7+8+9 = 45, i.e.4+5 = 9). 666 is the number of man and hidden meaning of this number 9 (666) is the greatest mysteries of occultism and theology. Hence number 9 is the luckiest number; as when multiplied by any number, it always reproduces itself. Hence it is indestructible and eternal.

9x8=72=7+2=9

9x7=63=6+3=9

9x6=54=5+4=9

9x5=45=4+5=9

9x4=36=3+6=9

9x3=27=2+7=9

9x2=18=1+8=9

9x8+9x7+9x6+9x5 = 72+63+54+45 = 234 = 2+3+4 = 9. Thus Number 9, whenever multiplied by any number repeats itself. It is the number of completeness and high achievement as it is the last and highest of the series from 1-9.

Further a circle has 360 degrees (3+6+0 = 9).

I have purposely referred to Colin Wilson, Cheiro and the Bible to highlight the importance of number 9, as the sole number of the occult, theology and metaphysical wisdom.The Chinese sages also considered number '9' as the number of Heaven. For the Chinese, a particular number is linked to the fate of a person consulting the I-Ching.

There is a story about Mao Zedog, who ruled over the Communist China for 41 years, i.e. from 1935 to 1976. He banned and denounced 'I-Ching' as it bred superstitions and was the relic of feudalism. But surprisingly enough, he did believe in its accurate predictions. Once at the advice of his son, he consulted an old fortune teller. On seeing the great leader, the astrologer started trembling. But when Mao persisted in his request, the fortune teller wrote the number 8341. Mao wanted to know what this number signified in his career. The fortune teller simply told him that only God knows the mystery of this number. This weird prediction came out to be true. Mao who was born on Dec. 26, 1893 died at the age of 83, i.e. on Sept. 9, 1976. Thus 83 was that mysterious number which fore-told his death at the age of 83. Further 41 indicated that his rule would end after 41 years of domination of China.

Cheiro who had studied the Hindu, Egyptian and Chaldeon system of 'Numerology' had predicted the exact dates and years of the coronation and death of King Edward VII. He had told the King that number 6 and 9 were very important in his life and he therefore might leave this world at the age of 69.

Here is another example. King Louis XVI of France was warned to be careful of the fatal number 21 of every month. He along with his queen, Marie

Antoinette, was arrested on June 21,1791, and both were guillotined on July 21,1793.

Numbers do have favourable or adverse impact on our lives. I have cited these instances for academic discussion and to highlight the significance of numbers in the life of a person. The main purpose of this book is to apprise the reader of the fortune telling aspect of I-Ching, but sometimes comparisons do bring out the finest aspects of the system. Should we call this fascination for numbers as Jung's "Synchronicity" or a "Coincidence" or the "Inexorable law of Providence"? But let me reiterate that "I-Ching is a divine lunar knowledge system conveyed in terms of inter-related symbols".

7

Sixty-four Hexagrams

Let us now come to brass, tacks and refer to the 'Divine Classic' for to interpret our fortunate or unfortunate times. It is indeed difficult to interpret the Hidden meaning embedded in the entails of this great book like precious gems. One has to dive deep into profoundest depths to collect such gems. I have, however, endeavoured in my way to interpret the words of wisdom after consulting innumerable books on the subject.

Before embarking upon the great venture, please study all the 64 Hexagrams, mentioned below. **Each Hexagram is read from bottom to top**.

I am just referring to the salient features of the Book of Change (I-Ching) and it should not be taken as a complete book, It requires a lot of further reading to be acquainted with its finest nuances. It may be regarded just a sketchy guide to enable the students of Chinese Astrology to go still further in their quest.

1. FIRST QIAN HEXAGRAM (Heaven)

This hexagram consists of six straight lines (all Yang), undivided, penetrating, firm and correct.

Comments

First Line: Dragon is asleep; no activity at all.

Second Line: Dragon appearing; meet him for benefits.

Third Line: Superior man active; carefree during day but a bit fearful in the evening.

Fourth Line: Dragon leaping and jumping.

Fifth Line: Dragon soaring in the sky; meet him to your advantage. Fifth place is the symbol of Heaven and hence is the exalted throne for the king.

Sixth Line: Dragon crossing all limits; hence dangerous situation.

Opinion

"Riding on six dragons, flying high towards heaven; the initiating is superior to all human beings, it is the symbol of the 'Superior man'. The ideal king or sage is Heaven and Heaven is the sage, i.e. He is the alter ego or another name of Heaven. God's in His Heaven meaning all's right with the world".

2. SECOND KUN HEXAGRAM (Earth)

(Responding answering; subordination or docility).

All six broken lines represent the symbol Yin. This Hexagram belongs to Earth. These divided lines are weak and hence they represent docility and submissiveness; but imbued with the firmness of a mare. Hence submissiveness or responding will be advantageous with fruitful results; whereas imitating or predetermining will lead to disastrous results.

Comment

In the 'Khien' (1st) trigram, there are only three undivided lines, i.e. Yang; whereas in 'Khwan' (2nd) trigram, there are six broken lines, i.e. Yin.

We find that Yang encompasses Yin too and its destiny number is 3+6 = 9 (both Yang and Yin added together). But the Yin does not enfold the Yang; hence its number remains as it is i.e. 6. Obviously 9 and 6 are used as numbers belonging to Yang and Yin.

Opinion

'Khien' (1st Hexagram) originates or initiates and 'Khwan' (2nd Hexagram) produces. With the intimate interaction of the two, i.e. Heaven and earth, beauty springs forth in the form of creation or fauna and flora. Naturally it refers to the limitless capacity of the earth to produce and nurture. Sky must chase, woo and court earth to impregnate it in order to create a more beautiful world.

I have earlier referred to the concept of Shiva and Shakti or 'Purusha and Prakriti' of Hindu mythology and Tantra. Without Shakti i.e. Mother earth, Shiva is just a non-entity. Creation needs both. Thus there appears an intimate co-relation between the Chinese concepts of Yang and Yin and Hindu mythology deities of Shiva and Shakti.

3. THE THIRD HEXAGRAM (Beginning)

(Strong and firm in the beginning and 5th place)

'Kun' is supposed to be the symbol of a struggling plant trying to come out of the entrails of the earth. Obviously it refers to the struggle and efforts of a state to come out of the period of chaos and anarchy.

Comments

Here we have two Yang symbols – one at the bottom and the other at the number 5. Being a Yang (-)

symbol, it represents firmness and correctness. The 5th Yang symbolises king's resolve to establish a beneficent and benign state where people will be prosperous and will live in peace and amity. All will be fine, if able and noble people are appointed to govern the people on behalf of the king.

Opinion

Here there is an oblique reference to the political and social turmoil and anarchy prevalent during those turbulent years. Only competent princes would retrieve the situation, but the king must not abdicate or shun his ordained duty and responsibility.

4. THE FOURTH HEXAGRAM (Childhood)

(Inexperienced and ignorant child or lad; strong at 2nd place and submissive at 5th place)

Comments

"I do not go and seek the inexperienced and ignorant lad, But it is he who comes and seeks me. Sincerity pays;

But if he applies 2nd or 3rd time, I shall refuse to teach him".

The first Yin (—) refers to shattering of ignorance and dispelling all doubts that shackle the mind. Hence it will be fruitful to use punishment.

The second Yang (-) teaches that the man must show patience with the inexperienced child. It will do a lot of good.

The third Yin (—) tells the wealthy not to marry an ambitious woman. The fourth Yin (- -) refers to chains of ignorance :

The fifth Yin (—) refers to the inexperienced and ignorant child. The top most Yang (-) being strong and firm suggests that no advantage will accrue by hitting the inexperienced youth. Try not to inflict injury upon him.

Opinion

The competent teacher, through hard measures, will bring about the best attributes, otherwise lying latent, of the ignorant youth to the fore, for good results. The service thus rendered will be emulated by the great.

5. THE FIFTH HEXAGRAM (Waiting or Needing):

▬▬ ▬▬
▬▬▬▬▬
▬▬ ▬▬
▬▬▬▬▬
▬▬▬▬▬
▬▬▬▬▬

(Strong, firm and confident at 5th place)

Here we have three Yang, followed by one Yin; one Yang and finally one Yin. All these denote that the bodies and souls require food for nourishment in order to sustain themselves.

Comments

The first three firm Yangs indicate that the subject is waiting on the border, the sandy beach of stream and mud near the stream. The fifth Yang presages that firmness will be advantageous and will bring good fortune, for the Yang at the fifth place is supreme and hence signifies victory, good luck and honor.

The fourth and sixth broken Yin indicates that the subject is waiting in a pool of blood and has entered the cave respectively. If he is hospitable to the three guests (the three warrior princes) and receives them with warmth and respect, he will be blessed with good fortune.

Opinion

With sincerity and fidelity or faith and firmness, one will achieve tremendous success and will be favoured by the Dame Fortune, after crossing all hurdles. By occupying an exalted position, assigned by Heaven, subject is, in fact, firm, correct, strong, and confident with profound faith.

The strong man, like Julius Caesar, is more dangerous than danger itself, but unlike him he is not rash, he restrains himself and waits for the most opportune moment to dare the devil at its den.

6. THE SIXTH HEXAGRAM (Contending)

(Strong at 5th place – symbol of ruler)

We find two Yins (at 1st and 3rd places) and four firm and strong Yangs at 2nd, 4th, 5th and 6th places.

The first Yin is, of course, weak and the subject is likely to be hurt in the scuffle. The 2nd Yin at the 3rd place indicates that the subject is weak and should remain in hiding at a safe place to appear at the opportune moment though the situation is hazardous and beset with dangers, yet it may lead to good fortune later. The 1st Yang at 2nd place expresses strength and firmness, but that strong resolve is weakened, being sandwiched between two weak Yins must therefore, retreat for tactical reasons.

The 2nd Yang at 4th place indicates that the subject is nowhere in reckoning; but the next Yang at 5th place being the symbol of king is firm and contending ultimately leading to good luck.

The last Yang reveals that the subject may be honoured by the king, in the form of a leather belt, but the honour is subsequently withdrawn.

Opinion

The values or virtues set forth by the great man are correct and hence his decision on all matters of contention will certainly be right. Further strength without the resolve to face the danger will not produce contention, and danger or peril without strength will also fail to contend fight.

7. THE SEVENTH HEXAGRAM (Common people or multitude)

(Strong at 2nd place alone)

The 1st, 3rd, 4th, 5th and 6th divided Yins reveal the host the following rules

(1) The host having incompetent leaders.

(2) The retreating host.

(3) The eldest are leading the multitude and the younger ones performing their assigned task.

(4) The great king distributing portfolios among his own men.

The 2nd Yang shows the leader among the multitude which envisages good fortune.

Comments

The leader or the superior man is solicitous of the welfare of the masses. There will be good fortune, if the superior man acts with firmness and magnanimity for the multitudes.

Opinion

The multitude or the masses are obedient to the General. War wreaks havoc and destroys the very fabric of the society, but the masses are ever ready to face all hazards for the sake of their king whom they all love and hold in great esteem.

8. THE EIGHTH HEXAGRAM (Union or attachment)

(Strong on the 5th position)

The 1st, 2nd, 3rd, 4th, and 6th Yin symbols reveal the subject showing :

(1) Sincerity to woo and win.

(2) Movement towards union.

(3) Seeking of union.

(4) Seeking union with someone beyond himself.

(5) Seeking union haphazardly without taking the above mentioned steps.

The 5th Yang symbol reveals firmness and correctness. It is the best example of seeking union or attachment. It presages good fortune.

Comments

Mutual assistance; seeking union or attachment, firm, straight and preserving, hence best luck.

Opinion

The inferiors are assembling around the superiors seeking support and union. The superior man, in his turn embraces the inferiors and bestows favours upon them.

9. THE NINTH HEXAGRAM (Small Restraint or Little Accumulation)

(Docility and submissiveness at 4th place)

The 1st, 2nd, 3rd, 5th and the 6th Yang firm and strong symbols reveal :

(1) The subject following his own destined course; hence good fortune.

(2) Good fortune.

(3) Husband and wife angling at each other with averted eyes.

(4) 4th Yin symbol – the subject is sincere; sincerity averts bloodshed.

(5) Sincerity of the subject.

(6) Falling of rain; wife exercising restraint is in a perilous state. Superior is forbidden to stick to his rigid position; evil will befall.

Comment

Under certain conditions, there will be prosperity, success and propensity; the little occupies the throne and all above and below it, obey the Ruler.

Opinion

Dense and dark clouds do shower rain and the rain of benevolent and beneficent government must descend upon all benefiting them without any consideration of caste or creed. Blessed rain like Mercy is doubly blessed – it blesses the benevolent ruler as well as the recipients.

10. THE TENTH HEXAGRAM (Fulfillment)

(Docile at 3rd position and strong and firm at 5th place)

Here we find the 3rd and the only Yin sandwiched between two Yang symbols, i.e. 1st and 2nd and 4th, 5th and 6th.

The Yang symbols express:

(1) The subject following the trodden path.

(2) Treading the easy path.

(3) The 3rd Yin symbol – a one-eyed man and a lame man limping his way – both think they can clearly see and walk perfectly over tiger's tail; full of sheer bravado; hence bad luck.

(4) Trampling over a tiger's tail cautiously, hence good luck.

(5) Firm and resolute.

(6) Scanning of the whole trodden path; good luck.

Comments

Perform your assigned task; and have the satisfaction of fulfillment. Let no feeling of guilt overpower you, as you are the ruler who must dispense justice. The Hero is treading over the tail of a tiger which is not a man-eater and which does not maul the rider. Hence success and good luck in all duties.

Opinion

Both the strong and weak symbols must be respected to have the satisfaction of fulfillment.

11. THE ELEVENTH HEXAGRAM (We see / Advance)

(The little gone and the great coming. Strong at the 2nd position and weak or submissive at 5th position)

(1) First Yang reveals the uprooting of grass along with its stem and roots. Naturally it refers to Advance, i.e. good fortune.

(2) The subject acts according to his inner urges as per the 2nd Yang.

(3) The 3rd Yang represents abiding peace; subject is not liable to err; hence no occasion for remorse and therefore an abiding mood of rejoicing.

(4) The 4th Yin reveals the diffidence on the part of the subject for not having confidence on his own resources – material and metal.

(5) The 5th Yin suggests great fortune.

(6) The 6th Yin suggests that the subject may have to rue and regret his decision.

Comments

The top, i.e. three Yangs is supporting the bottom, i.e. three Yins. Obviously there will be abundance of everything and good fortune will rule. It will be a state of supreme bliss, for it connotes blessed union of Heaven and Earth. Harmonious interaction with the heaven and Earth augurs well for the state and the people. It results in peace, profundity, prosperity and all round bliss. The little of course is leaving and the great is entering.

Opinion

The Heaven and the Earth cohabit and have interaction to produce beauty, peace and prosperity. The upper and the lower must unite in a close embrace for the best results. Let us call it the ecstasy of 'Love chase'. Earth can not escape the sky; let it flee up or down, the sky flows into it and makes it fruitful, whether it wills or not.

12. THE TWELFTH HEXAGRAM (Obstruction or Hindrance)

(Submissive at 2nd position and strong at 5th position)

This is the reverse of Tai 11th Hexagram. Here, unlike the 11th Hexagram, the Earth rests over the Heaven every thing goes topsy-turvy and awry. It alludes to the exit of the great and entrance of the small.

(1) The 1st Yin refers to the complete eradication of grass along with its stress and roots. Only perseverance and firmness will pay.

(2) (2) The 2nd Yin – the subject is pertinent, docile & submissive.

(3) The 3rd Yin suggests that the subject is ashamed and full of remorse.

(4) The 4th Yang refers to the subject being faithful following the dictates of heaven.

(5) The 5th Yang is the most firm and refers to the end of grief and hindrance, i.e. harbinger of happiness.

(6) The 6th Yang refers to the complete annihilation of the situation of grief, unhappiness and obstruction, i.e. situation of complete bliss and joy.

Comments

The great is gone; the little enters. Earth and Heaven are no longer in harmony. Chaotic situation may prevail as all links between the states are either snapped or are not functioning properly. They may ultimately lead to misfortune.

Opinion

In Nature, it is the Heaven who initiates and not the Earth, which only responds. To remedy the chaotic situation the upper, i.e. the nobles will have to take the initiative in embracing the lower, i.e. the masses and not vice-versa.

13. THE THIRTEENTH HEXAGRAM (Union of Men/ Harmonious relationship)

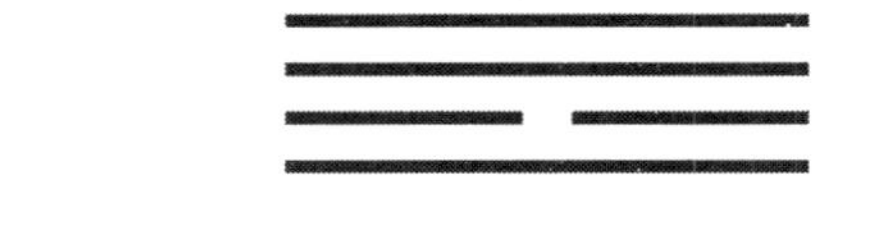

(Docile or yielding at the 2nd position and strong at 5th position)

(1) The 1st Yang indicates the union of man, hence all correct.

(2) The 2nd Yin reveals that union with kith and kin; hence cause for regret.

(3) The 3rd, 4th, 5th and 6th Yang elements are firm; hence no cause of regret and remorse.

Comments

The only Yin symbol at 2nd place is soliciting to have union with five Yang symbols. A favorable situation is in the offing. The yielding is central and seeks harmonious union with the Heaven or the initiating; hence harmonious relationship.

14. THE FOURTEENTH HEXAGRAM (Great Having or Great Harvest)

(Yielding at 5th position)

There is a preponderance of Yang symbols, i.e. 1st, 2nd, 3rd, 4th and 6th are 5 Yang symbols. The 5th one is Yin. It indicates its sincerity to embrace all Yang symbols.

Comments

There will be tremendous progress, prosperity and success. Sincerity in a ruler is desirable, but he must inspire awe, fear and respect among his subject. Heaven approves such arrangement; hence it derives the name of Great Having or Great Harvest.

Opinion

The ruler must direct all his actions judiciously and intelligently to win over the subjects. This is what the seasons of Heaven demand and dictate.

15. THE FIFTEENTH HEXAGRAM (Humbleness)

(Yang strong at the 3rd position)

The only Yang symbol is at the 3rd place. Naturally a Yang line at this place is weak and inauspicious; but this Yang becomes the most auspicious because of his humility. Although sandwiched between Yin elements, the superior man will be the harbinger of good fortune and success. It should be remembered that in such an adverse situation, humility pays.

Opinion

There is reference to setting of sun and waning of Moon, after they have run their full allotted course. Even the Earth passes through the vagaries of season. On the spiritual side it refers to the best effect of Humility.

16. THE SIXTEENTH HEXAGRAM (Happy contentment / Delight / Harmony)

(Yang strong at 4th place)

Here we find one Yang symbol at 4th place wedged between Yin symbols at 1, 2, 3, 5 and 6 positions. The 1st Yin reveals subject's delight and contentment. The 2nd Yin declares the subject as firm and steadfast as a rock. The 3rd Yin reveals that the subject is soliciting favours while indulging in a feeling of delights. The only Yang symbol is at 4th place sandwiched among Yin symbols. It shows from what source he receives delight and satisfaction.

The 5th Yin represents someone suffering from a chronic ailment or complaint. The 6th or the topmost Yin reveals a darkened mind addicted to sense of delight.

Comments

While remaining and acting in unison with the times, the only firm Yang, is filled with delight. All the five Yin symbols respond favourably to it.

Opinion

Obedience is the greatest virtue. There does exist harmony between natural phenomena and human life like the one between the heaven and the Earth so one ought to live in unison with the times – whether turbulent or happy and auspicious.

17. THE SEVENTEENTH HEXAGRAM (following)

(Yang firm at the 1st place)

1. First Yang firm at the initial stage; tells us the subject is changing the object of pursuit; but firmness will be advantageous.
2. The 2nd and 3rd Yin elements show that adherence to following will yield best results.
3. The 4th Yang .efers to evil though to be firm.
4. The 5th Yang refers to good fortune, if he be sincere in fostering and following.
5. The 6th Yin refers to sincerely firmly held.

Comments

The firm Yang submits itself cheerfully to the 'yielding', i.e. three Yins. The docility offers it delight and pleasure.

Opinion

Respect for those placed at a higher pedestal and giving to those following. Union of these two, i.e. excitement of motion and pleasure produces the best results.

18. THE EIGHTEENTH HEXAGRAM (Remedying of Painful and Troublesome Services)

He, who deals firmly and properly will, of course, meet with success after initial hurdles such as crossing the stream. He must judiciously weigh his options three days before the turning point and three days after too.

The 1st Yin refers to the troubles caused by the father. The son, if capable, will save the father from ignominy and humiliation.

The 2nd Yang refers to the problems faced by the son created by his mother.

The 3rd Yang again shows the son grappling with the problems created by the father.

The 4th Yin reveals the son looking indulgently at the problems caused by the father.

The 5th Yin again refers to the troubles caused by the father.

The 6th Yang reveals the one who does not serve his master, but looks after his own affairs, i.e. an egoist.

Comments

Every ending leads to a new beginning. There is continuity that shall never end. This is what Heaven demands and this is the supreme will of Heaven. You will find firm Yang at the top and yielding Yin at the bottom. Three days are quite significant. The state is in utter decay and disarray, remedial measures are urgently required. Hence the Remedying Hexagram.

Opinion

Old order must change giving way to a new one. History indeed is a narrative of change. One must remedy the situation to move ahead and not to remain stagnant.

19. THE NINETEENTH HEXAGRAM (Approach of Authority or Approaching)

(Strong at the initial and 2nd place)

Lin actually means 'Great'. It also signifies the approach of the 'Powers that be the king' with a view to examining, inspecting, confronting and ruling over the subjects. Here we have two Yang symbols at the 1st and 2nd places. They signify the advance of the subject with firmness; hence presaging good fortune. They are followed by four Yin elements. They indicate the advance of wisdom, sincerity, befitting a great monarch. They all will be the harbinger of good fortune. In short it means Approaching. The strong and firm Yangs are growing in wisdom and advancing in the highest style to a period of good fortune.

20. THE TWENTIETH HEXAGRAM (Sharing / Manifesting or Contemplating / Watching into the Distance)

(Two firm and strong Yang symbols at 5th stage and top)

This hexagram can be interpreted as contemplating or watching or manifesting or showing. In simple words it tells us how the monarch manifests himself before his people and how they watch him.

The two upper firm Yang lines refer to the royal authority vested in the king and four weak Yin lines refer to the ministers, masses and other officers serving under the sole authority and patronage of the king.

Comments

This Hexagram reveals that the devotee has washed his hands or performed sacred oblation but has not made offering with devotion and sincerity and reverence. The greatest virtue in the king is to be a sincere worshipper. This superior man is not exempt from the duty of self-examination or contemplation i.e. he must watch his actions. All the habitants of this Earth are obliged to follow the laws of Heaven.

Opinion

Inexorable and mysterious are the ways of Providence and every one howsoever powerful will have to abide by them.

21. THE TWENTY-FIRST HEXAGRAM (Union by Gnawing or Eradicating)

This Hexagram literally means 'Union by gnawing'. We find two firm and strong 'Yang' lines at the top and the bottom; while all other lines except the 4th one are divided and weak. In other words the 1st, 4th

& 6th lines are firm and strong whereas the 2nd, 3rd & 5th lines are divided and broken in the middle.

The hexagram ostensibly appears like a jaw or mouth with something stuck between them to keep it open. Let us call it, obstruction. The 4th firm line can be termed as obstruction. Let that be eradicated to close the mouth.

Comments

Eradicate the obstacle that hampers the union. These obstacles can only be removed by the use of force and coercion or by clemency. This force is represented by gnawing or eradicating, i.e. by legal constraints. The results will be auspicious and favourable for all the nobles as well as the commons. This is the only *Mantra* for all round success.

Opinion

Judgment must be tempered with mercy and leniency. The quality of mercy is not strained. It drops as the gentle rain from heaven.

It is twice blessed. It blessed him that gives and him that takes. Judgment must, therefore, be mollified by Mercy; and that is the greatest attribute of a monarch.

22. THE TWENTY-SECOND HEXAGRAM (Ornamental or Adorning)

(Firm at the top and giving or yielding at same spot)

This hexagram is ornamental in nature and obviously in society too.

The 1st firm Yang reveals beautifying or adorning the feet; the 2nd weak Yin adorns the beard.

The 3rd Yang reveals that the subject is adorned with rich favours. The 2nd and 3rd lines (Yin and Yang) are the adornment of beard and chin. The 4th weak Yin reveals as if it is adorned; but in white colour. The 5th weak Yin shows the subject as miserly but leading to good fortune.

The 6th strong Yin shows that there is no error – and it is returning pure, white, initial simplicity.

Comments

The Yin in the middle adorns the firm Yang and the firm Yang at the top adorns the yielding. It also signifies that ornament in nature should be imbibed in society, but it should be subservient to what is substantial. There should be free course, but there will be no advantage, if allowed to be the leader.

23. THE TWENTY-THIRD HEXAGRAM
(Falling or Causing to Fall)

(Firm at the top only)

We see only one Yang element in the Hexagram. The other five Yin symbols are moving upwards. Their intention is just to overthrow and destroy the only Yang symbol. This Hexagram symbolises falling or causing to fall. It is broadly applicable to both the natural and political domains. It refers to the process of decay or overthrow. In simple words it means the mean and vile men are gradually overthrowing the noble and the good; but the firm at the top place is the only saving grace. Let him remain firm and wait for the better times.

The 1st Yin symbol refers to the injury to the legs by overthrowing the couch. The 2nd Yin refers to the injury to the frame.

The 3rd Yin also refers to the complicity of the subject with the first two conspirators.

The 4th Yin refers to evil in the intentions of the rebel.

The 5th refers to the advantage what may finally accrue. Here there is a change of symbol.

The 6th firm and strong Yang withstands all attacks from the 1st four Yin and regains his strength and aura.

Comments

The schemes ultimately fail and the people love their monarch who has survived the sinister attempts of his foes. It is the inexorable laws of nature that spring follows winter and sunshine after dark clouds. If winter comes, can spring be far behind? Obviously the bright period of turning back comes after the dark period of falling away.

Opinion

The fundamental laws of nature having a bearing on political and social life of a country. 'Rise and fall' and 'fall and rise' are the laws of nature and society too. The Bible says, "In quietness and confidence shall be thy strength".

24. THE TWENTY-FOURTH HEXAGRAM (Coming Back / Returning)

This hexagram is the symbol of 'Returning'. In the previous Hexagram (23), we have noticed the inferior overpowering the superior before evil.

It must be remembered that change is the law of nature and the old order changes, yielding place to anew. After perfection comes decay. When the evil reaches the top of graph, it starts sliding down then the truth and good triumphs over the evil. Here we have only one strong and firm Yang symbol in the initial place followed by five weak Yin lines.

Comments

The strong element will not meet any resistance from the weak lines, when he returns. His return will be smooth as the five Yin elements will extend the hand of friendship. The firm Yang will grow into prosperity and every thing will be fine under the heaven and over the earth. In simple words, the firm return, and its bright quality will shine more and more.

Opinion

The mind of Heaven and Earth constitutes love for life and beauty together with goodness that rules over the whole of nature.

25. THE TWENTY-FIFTH HEXAGRAM
(Simple and Sincere/ Without Falsehood)

This hexagram indicates that subject is simple, sincere, without an iota of falsehood in him. Honesty or freedom from deceit is the basic attribute of Heaven and goodness in humanity.

Here we have firm Yang elements at the initial and 5th spots.

The 1st firm element suggests that the subject is sincere and free from all falsehood.

The 2nd weak symbol refers to the advantage and success.

The 3rd weak element suggests calamity befalling the subject. The 4th strong Yang talks of caution & life of rectitude.

The 5th Yang however, is the strongest and refers to element of sincerity in the subject which will offer him joy and happiness.

The topmost Yang again refers to sincerity and life full of happiness and advantages ahead.

Comments

Sincerity will ultimately pay. Truth should be practised from the beginning to the end. Great prosperity and happiness will be the outcome of such a course of rectitude, firmness and correct behaviour. This is what Heaven desires. The message is clear:one may suffer an unexpected bad patch in his life, though no fault of his. Let him submit himself to the supreme will of Heaven and resign himself to his fate. There lies his deliverance; but under no circumstance he should leave the path of rectitude, truth and sincerity. This is what all ancient sages and scriptures teach.

Let me quote from *'The Gita'*, the most sacred of all Hindu scriptures:

> *"My devote does work for Me;*
> *Selfless, unattached with malice to none;*
> *For him, I am the supreme goal of life;*
> *And he ever remains friendly to everyone".*

It means that we must resign ourselves to Him and do our ordained duty.

The very meaning of Islam is also *'Obedience to Allah'* and submission to His supreme will.

26. THE TWENTY- SIXTH HEXAGRAM (Great Accumulation)

This symbol has two meanings, i.e. 'restrained' as well as 'accumulation'. In simple words it means that what is harassed or repressed do accumulate their strength and virtue. Different lines refer to repression.

The 1st three lines are the recipient of that repression and the top three wield the authority for that repression. Naturally it leads to the accumulation of virtue and strength; hence it is named as 'great accumulation'.

Comments: You find here firm or strong Yang element at the top place. It teaches us the lesson of firmness in accumulating virtue, despite great coercion and repression. Such a person, through tenacity and courage in face of heavy odds, will be able to enjoy the ruler's patronage and will achieve tremendous success even in most difficult tasks.

I remember a Persian verse in this context:

"When a cat is repressed beyond certain limits, it becomes so desperate that it takes out the leopard's eyes with its paws. This may also be called great accumulation of strength after being coerced and restrained.

Opinion

It evidently refers to the 'grand accumulation of virtue and substantial solidity inherent in mountains. Obviously the good and the noble will not be ignored and left in adversity, because they have the accumulated strength to fight back.

27. THE TWENTY- SEVENTH HEXAGRAM (Nourishing)

This hexagram is the symbol of mouth or jaw; hence the name 'nourishing'. It refers to nourishing of the body, or mind or the whole being. The process of nourishment should be harmonious, correct and in accordance with the norms prescribed by the sages. The 1st and the topmost lines are firm and sandwiched between them are four weak divided lines. The topmost being the strongest, suggests the subject is in a position to command and rule. Responsibility, of course, is big but with nourishment and of virtues from the Heaven, the Earth, the ancient sages and from all auspicious corners of the universe, the subject can surmount all such problems, howsoever, insurmountable.

"All must perform the work of nourishing the people".

28. THE TWENTY- EIGHTH HEXAGRAM (Extraordinary or Great Exceeding)

Here in this Hexagram, we find firm Yang lines at the 2nd spot and at the 5th place. But when we study the whole Hexagram, we find two weak divided lines at the bottom and the top and four firm lines between them. It means that the beam is unable to support itself and may fall. However the 2nd and 5th strong and firm lines do hold it. Ultimate consequence of all these lines is that though the beam is weak and unsustainable, yet there will be a definite advantage in moving to any direction.

Opinion

Wood here is the natural symbol of Sun and flexibility attributed to the sun is of paramount importance. Thus flexibility is the guiding principle of this Hexagram.

29. THE TWENTY-NINTH HEXAGRAM (Pit or Perilous Cavity or Pitch Darkness):

The very meaning of this hexagram – a dangerous and dark pit, with water flowing through it – symbolises danger ahead. With sincerity and penetrating mind, it can be encountered and finally surmounted. One can get out of this dark hell through sheer grit, firmness and tenacity of purpose and invincible heart and mind.

Here we have a firm straight line at 2nd spot and one at the 5th place too. The other four lines are broken and weak.

Comments

Darkness of the pit with water flowing through it is aggravated, i.e. it becomes pitch dark. There are dangers ahead lurking to pounce upon the subject. One must rely upon one's own strength, firmness, sincerity and above all tenacity of heart and invincibility of mind. Honours await such a man. His motto should be excelsior, i.e. to go forward in order to snatch victory and success from the jaws of danger. There is always light after the dark tunnel.

Opinion

There is a saying that water stops at the proper time and also moves at the proper time. This, of course, is the chief attribute of a superior man.

30. THE THIRTIETH HEXAGRAM (Brightness / Intelligence)

The very name of this hexagram signifies fire and light with the Sun as the chief source emanating light and flooding the world with brightness. Let us call the fire and light of the sun as double brightness.

Here we have four strong straight lines at the initial, 3rd, 4th and 6th spots; whereas the weak divided lines (i.e. yielding) are at the 2nd and 5th places.

Comments

The 1st line being strong ascends upwards but his path is beset with danger. He must be careful in his venture.

2nd weak line, occupies the centre.

The 3rd strong line suggests that the setting sun's light is becoming dim.

The 4th firm line suggests disaster.

The 5th line, though occupying central position of honour, is weak. With humility and correctness of behaviour, he will have good luck and success.

The 6th firm line signifies munificence, light and vigour. The 'double brightness' shows the path even in darkness.

Just as light dispels darkness, the subject can sift the grain from the chaff or distinguish right from wrong or good from evil. One can retrieve one's luck and change the bad into good or a negative situation into a positive one. Hindu scriptures also teach – *"from darkness unto light"*.

Opinion

Double brightness refers to the king becoming brighter and brighter, i.e. achieving great heights of glory and power with the passage of time.

31. THE THIRTY FIRST HEXAGRAM
(Mutual Influence / Jointly)

People have interpreted the above hexagram differently, but the most acceptable and plausible interpretation is that the weak and yielding is at the top and the firm is at the 3rd spot. It is true that they are not occupying any central position; but their placement in correct positions and their mutual response and influence upon each other is remarkable.

Comments

The submissive or docile is at the top and the firm is below. It indicates that a perfect union has been established and the neutral influence or love is advantageous to both. Love is thus the building force.

Opinion

The very meaning of the hexagram is mutual influence, which inter alia implies love, confidence and, above all, satisfaction. When two opposing but complementary forces of yielding Yin and initiating Yang unite into one soul and two bodies, its effect is mutually beneficial to both and all their progeny. It is a case of marriage with a young lady after performing all the sacred rituals enjoined by the scriptures and ancient traditions. Such a marriage is indeed effective and long-lasting, which brings prosperity and conjugal happiness to both the husband and wife. Heaven and earth unite and harmonious transformation takes place for the betterment of all.

Even in India such marriages are solemnised with the blessings of the parents, priests and social organisations. Since such marriages have social sanctions; the husband and wife are bound by mutual affection till death. Such marriages indeed are made and sanctioned in Heaven.

32. THE THIRTY- SECOND HEXAGRAM (Perseverance / long-lasting)

This hexagram is the symbol of perseverance or long-lasting. It is firm Yang at the 2nd spot; which indicates that there is no longer any occasion for regret and remorse. The strong and firm Yang at the 2nd spot and the weak one in the initial stage, i.e. just below it, connote thunder and wind. There is mutual and beneficial communication between the two, i.e. they both have the attributes of strength or firmness of the Yang and submissiveness and docility of the Yin.

Comments

The relationship between the husband and wife should be of mutual trust and should continue till the last breath. This relationship should be strengthened and cemented as the time rolls on and must be 'long lasting'. That is the message of this hexagram.

Opinion

Here the Yin, i.e. wife occupies the lowest spot; hence should be paradigm of submissiveness, virtue and docility. The husband, i.e. Yang being firm and superior must be affectionate towards her. Here lies the secret of 'Long-lasting' marriage and a strong social fabric. All the scriptures of the world–whether Chinese, Hindu, Islamic or Christians–preach the gospel of mutual and long-lasting relationship between the couples. This hexagram should be read in continuance with the previous one, i.e. no. 31 of mutual influence.

33. THE THIRTY- THIRD HEXAGRAM (Tactical Retreat or Retiring)

This hexagram, if read carefully, indicates the advance and domination of unscrupulous and inferior forces to the detriment of the right and superior man. The latter must retreat in order to regain their strength – physical as well as moral. This will enable them to hit back and regain the lost ground. Let us call it tactical retreat.

This 'tactical retreating' is owing to the advance of two Yin lines at the bottom which are powerful enough to force the Yang elements to fall back.

Opinion

The retreat does not necessarily adversely reflect upon the prowess and bravery of the retiring superior man. It is, of course, an admirable retreat and is aimed at replenishing the lost strength. It is foolhardy to fight against an advancing superior force of unscrupulous enemies. Tactical retreat is the best weapon against formidable but wily foe.

34. THE THIRTY- FOURTH HEXAGRAM (Abundance of Vigour or Great Strength)

In this hexagram, we find four predominant strong Yang lines. It is the symbol of strength, valour and authority but the ruler wielding such great power should not be rudely aggressive, self-opinionated and callous towards those over whom he rules. This strength should be tempered with right conduct and right behaviour.

Comments

The strong Yang at the 4th spot refers to the chieftain or the head of country. Being in a dominant position, he must show magnanimity and large-heartedness. Don't we say 'He who is great should be upright'? This righteousness is in direct proportion to the greatness of the monarch.

Opinion

All the scriptures teach us the lesson of humanity and compassion. The *Holy Quran*, the sacred book of Muslims, says, *"Praise be to Allah who is the Lord of all the worlds! And who is the most beneficent, kind and compassionate"*. When the Lord of the entire world, i.e. God is kind and merciful, why shouldn't the rulers of this world be? The greater the man, the greater the desire for uprighteous conduct. This is the only truth sanctioned by Heaven and Earth. A fruit-laden tree always bends, thus uprighteous, correct behaviour, magnanimity, etc. are the virtues found in great measure in all great men.

35. THE THIRTY- FIFTH HEXAGRAM (Advancing / Moving Ahead)

Comments

The docile and submissive Yin at the 5th spot occupies the central place. Here we have the image of the sun traversing the sky and brightening the Earth with its effulgence. This hexagram, in fact, refers to a feudal prince who was able to win the king's confidence and love through meritorious services. Such are the virtues and noble attributes of the prince who advances ahead of other compatriots and colleagues because of his intrinsic worth. We can compare his advancement to the brilliant light of the sun during the whole of the day. In other words its brilliance increases manifold as the sun traverses the whole of sky from the east to the west.

Opinion

The brightness appears over the sky which is radiated by the Earth. The gentle and the docile is moving ahead and advancing towards its cherished goal despite a few trivial impediments in the initial stages.

36. THE THIRTY-SIXTH HEXAGRAM (Intelligence Wounded or Brilliance Injured and Suffocated)

Here we find two most important positions, i.e. the 2nd and the 5th spot occupied by weak and yielding Yin symbols. They refer to the times of complete darkness from which ensues misery and hardship. In other words they represent wounded or repressed brilliance.

This hexagram also refers to a competent and noble officer serving an incompetent weak and unsympathetic monarch. Now the pesky question arises as to how such an officer should conduct himself in the presence of a weakling lord.

Opinion

This hexagram can be interpreted in the Chinese axiom: *"Hiding one's brilliance and biding one's adverse time patiently waiting for the good days"*. During adversity and dark days, one must wait for the opportune moment to retrieve the glorious position.

"Keep your cool, when the barbs of misfortune hit you". That should be the motto.

"If winter comes, can spring be far behind? Dark clouds of misery will ultimately disappear, and the sun will again shine". But there is a catch here: Don't rush; for hurry will spoil your chances of regaining your lost glory or 'injured brilliance'.

'Fools rush in where angels fear to tread', imbibe this lesson.

'Wait and wait patiently' should be the chief *mantra*.

37. THE THIRTY-SEVENTH HEXAGRAM (A Household or the Family)

This hexagram refers to the harmonious relationship between the husband and the wife to run the household smoothly and to the advantage of all the members of the family. We find in this hexagram the yielding element of Yin at the 2nd place and the firm and strong Yang at the 5th place. The firm element means husband and the yielding element connotes wife. The husband and wife must be supreme in their own respective spheres ordained by the sages and social norms.

Opinion

Harmony in the couple's relationship is the greatest desideratum in the smooth running of the household. Lack of harmony and love will ruin and shatter the family. Both husband and wife must cooperate in the performance of their respective roles, as ordained by the society. In simple words the 'firmness' symbolised by men, and 'gentleness' symbolised by wife should coordinate themselves to make the home a veritable heaven of love, affection and peace. This time-tested formula is applicable to the ruler and the subjects too.

Even in Indian families the harmony in the relationship between wife and husband is the greatest cementing factor in making the house a 'real home', where peace and love reign supreme.

38. THE THIRTY- EIGHTH HEXAGRAM (Diversity)

If division or mutual distrust prevails in a society, we must endeavour to mend the fences and heal the wounds inflicted by trying to revamp and purge the whole system of the divisive elements. In other words, where there is diversity, we should try to bring about union within diversity. Let the mutual acrimony and alienation be cured through rapprochement and general consensus. Alienation, mistrust, wrangles and bickering are a natural sequence in every family. Thus there is a great need for common virtue regulating the household having girls from diverse families and environments.

Opinion

The submissive Yin is at the 5th place which responds well to the firm Yang at the 2nd place. The 'yielding' element is advancing upwards to attain harmonious blending with the 'firm'. Hence need for harmony and general agreement among diverse elements in a family.

39. THE THIRTY- NINTH HEXAGRAM (Hardship or Difficulties)

Here in the hexagram we notice a firm and strong Yang element in the 5th spot. 'Kien' (39) refers to the weakness in the legs and feet; obviously it means difficulty in walking and advancing. One should, in such circumstances, adopt a posture of 'prudent caution'. This element of prudence is recommended for the king who is facing an uphill task in running the government and controlling the officers.

Opinion

The firm Yang element is placed at the 5th spot which, inter-alia, means the great personage. Through prudence and caution, the king can overcome all the hardships which hamper his advancement. He must take advantage of every opportunity and shun those entire elements who pose difficulties in the performance of his royal duties.

40. THE FORTIETH HEXAGRAM (Relief or Untying the Knot)

We referred to difficulties and hardships in the previous hexagram; now let us talk of getting relief from all those problems. This hexagram is the symbol of loosening or getting rid of all obstructions and complications and seeing a clear sunshine ahead. 'From darkness unto light'; so say the Hindu scriptures too.

The advantage will accrue in moving to the south-west. Its meaning is the same as returning to old conditions, i.e. ushering in a period of good fortune if early operations are conducted.

Opinion

Here the yielding element Yin is positioned at the 5th place and the firm Yang is at the 2nd spot. It clearly states that if a modest and submissive ruler has competent ministers and officers to handle the affairs of the states, all his worries will be over. He, in other words, will be relieved of all hardships previously faced. The yielding Yin at 5th place is symbol of a humble monarch and the firm Yang at 2nd place connotes competent minister to aid the king in discharging his royal tasks. 'After a bad patch comes great sunshine'; this is the fundamental law of nature.

41. THE FORTY- FIRST HEXAGRAM (Decreasing or Diminishing)

In this Hexagram we find the yielding Yin element at the 5th place. The lower is the symbol of the masses and the above is indicative of the position of a king.

The nature and society must perform the balancing act, in order to keep everything in right perspective. This is the fundamental law of balance, ordained by nature. If this balance is tilted this way or that way the results may be disastrous. The decreasing or diminishing must be replenished and the increasing must be decreased. In simple words those whose coffers are overflowing must be stripped of the extra flab and those who need more, must be compensated or their depleted coffer must be filled. This is absolutely essential to maintain balance between decreasing and increasing, in order to bring all to a level playing field.

Opinion

James Leggie has interpreted it as follows:

"Every diminution and repression of what we have in excess, to bring it in accordance with right and reason, is comprehended under sun. Let there be sincerity in doing this and it will lead to the happiest results".

To be precise those who have lot of wealth should be asked to fish out the extra pound to fill up the depleted basket of the lowly placed. Let there be sincerity in the whole transaction. This way the rich and the low will be mutually benefited. This is also the law of balance or fair taxation.

The strong and fabulously affluent will have to make a small sacrifice for the needy and the destitute. The strong should be diminished and the weak should be strengthened. This way the society will flourish and there will be peace and prosperity in the country. The hiatus between the rich and the poor will be diminished to a great extent.

42. THE FORTY- SECOND HEXAGRAM (Addition or Increasing)

This hexagram may be read in continuation with the previous one, i.e. the monarch should disperse justice and benefits of his munificence to all and add to the resources of the masses. Addition to the coffers of the lower and decrease in the coffers of the higher should be the chief *mantra* of the ruler.

Opinion

The insufficient must be compensated by those having their coffers full. Further to this, during the time of plenty don't feel elated and during adversity don't feel let down. Only the hollow men brag of their wealth and when they face adverse times, they lose their balance of mind. One must, therefore, save for the rainy day but should be large-hearted enough to help the weak when the going is fine.

43. THE FORTY- THIRD HEXAGRAM (To Eliminate or to Remove)

In this hexagram; we notice five firm Yang elements and one weak Yin element at the top. This clearly states that there is some powerful officer or minister who is weakening the very fabric of the state and society through corrupt practices. It is absolutely necessary to eliminate such a black sheep. The method to be applied should be the power of the character rather than force. This way the ruler will win the sympathy of the masses and will also be able to get rid of a corrupt officer.

Opinion

This hexagram refers to the power vested in people. In order to eliminate bad elements from the government, the king must seek the support of the people. He must not be actuated by any ill-will or a feeling of personal vendetta, but should have the welfare of his subjects at heart. Such corrupt officers occupying topmost positions in the government are like the termites eating away the very vitals of the state. The earlier they are removed, the better for everyone.

44. THE FORTY- FOURTH HEXAGRAM (Encountering or Unexpected Meeting or Appearance)

In this hexagram, we find the 1st Yin line as the symbol of a female who is audacious, over-bold and exceptionally strong. Though all other lines are strong and undivided – the symbols of male – yet the initial strong Yin overpowers and dominates them all. She will subdue and win all the five strong elements. Hence marriage with such a female will spell disaster and is, therefore, forbidden.

Opinion

The weak line unexpectedly encounters the strong ones and plays the principal role. The strong ones play subservient to her as if mesmerised by her strength and boldness. The decision is: The female is bold and strong and obviously such a marriage is not recommended.

45. THE FORTY- FIFTH HEXAGRAM
(Collecting or Bringing Together)

Here we find the firm and strong Yang at the fifth spot and the docile and yielding Yin at the 2nd place.

It indicates that a happy union exists between the monarch and his advisors or between the rich and the poor.

Opinion

There are two Yang elements that occupy exalted positions. Thus there exists a complete rapport between the king and his ministers. They are all working in unison to bring peace and prosperity amongst the various wings of the administration, which is absolutely necessary.

The king will leave for his ancestral palace and interact with the souls of his forefathers. This meeting of the souls will usher in a period of plenty, peace and success.

46. THE FORTY-SIXTH HEXAGRAM (Ascending or Advancing or Growing upwards)

In this hexagram, we find the weak yielding Yin at the initial spot and the initial spot is the fundamental root of growth. Every growth begins at the root and the tree ascends upwards. This hexagram refers to the advance of an officer from a lower to the higher position of eminence. But this firmness must be tempered with humility and modesty. Further the great man must 'advance southwards' which is another name for advancing upwards.

Opinion

The great man will advance further to attain an eminent position. In order to ascend, one must have a strong base or support. If the root is delicate, the tree will be delicate and weak too. Thus after happy union comes the 'upwards movement' to the advantage of all. A loner living in his own ivory tower, far from the human society, never ascends and succeeds in life. Both the hexagrams No.45 and 46 should be read together.

Progress and success will be assured if the subject advances towards southwards, which means all sunshine and glory.

47. THE FORTY- SEVENTH HEXAGRAM (Exhausting)

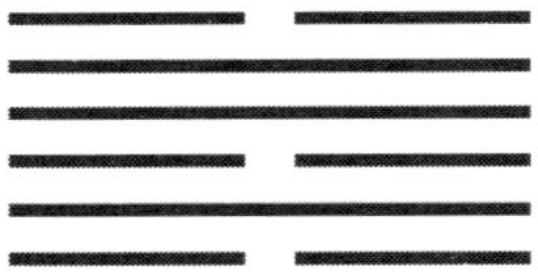

In this hexagram, we find the 2nd firm Yang is sandwiched between weak 1st and 3rd Yin, and 4th and 5th Yang elements which are the symbols of the ruler. His ministers are covered by the weak 6th Yin. All this indicates that the evil is triumphant over the good and all the good men are being trampled over by the evil forces.

This Hexagram also refers to the picture of a tree struggling to come out of its stifling enclosure; but ultimately withers and falls for want of a room and sufficient air.

Opinion

When the country is in shambles and the evil men rule the roost, the great man may falter. But by 'skilful management', he can recover the lost ground and usher in a new era of good fortune, good governance and prosperity. Mere words will not do. If he speaks, he will not be heard and believed. Hollow words will not convince the people. What is required is 'action' on the part of the great man. Even in adversity, the superior man does not lose his patience and takes remedial measures to retrieve the situation and change it from that of 'hopelessness' to a 'win win' situation.

48. THE FORTY- EIGHTH HEXAGRAM (Replenishing)

䷯

This hexagram has a message for the government and the message is conveyed through a well. A well is the source of nourishing water which refreshes the people. Men may change; societies may undergo transformation with the passage, but the well remains unchangeable. It is an eternal source of supply of water to men and lands. The barren lands are irrigated and the parched lips are satiated. The deeper the well, the more refreshing and nutritious is its water. The water is drawn in a bucket with the help of a pulley. So should be the case with government. Such a scenario was very common a few decades back even in rural China and India, too.

Opinion

A well with plenty of deep water used to be a source of nourishment and replenishment for the people of ancient China. The ideal government is the one which takes its cue from the parable of the well. The king, like the water of the well, must nourish and give all amenities to the masses who, in their turn, will love, adore and support the king. Water of the well never gets stale and stagnant. It is always a fresh and nourishing source of happiness.

49. THE FORTY- NINTH HEXAGRAM (Changing or Abolition of Old)

It is used here as a symbol of change. Change should not be abrupt and sudden as such a change may create suspicion in the minds of the people. It should be slow, gradual and methodical. So we must effect change with great caution.

Opinion:

The old, rickety and obsolete order must change with the passage of time. Change is the law of nature. It brings out freshness, new vigour and new life. It is the supreme will of Heaven as well and is therefore to the advantage of the people at large. If the water remains stationary, it stinks and become stagnant. Similar is the case with all social and political organisations. But the men, like the two great kings of ancient China must be wise, firm and strong. They must be trusted and must be made popular leaders of men during the period of such a transformation; otherwise they may witness great uprising and upheaval. Here are few lines from Confucius's comments on this hexagram of change.

"Heaven and earth abolish the old to usher a new world order;

The four seasons too complete such a change".

In simple words, people must support a revolution heralding prosperity, peace and change for the better. Let me also quote Tennyson in favour of change:

"The old order changeth, yielding place to new;

And God fulfills Himself in many ways".

50. THE FIFTIETH HEXAGRAM (Cauldron or Establishment of a New Order)

Ting actually means a cauldron. In ancient China, when a new monarch ascended the throne, the first thing he did was to promulgate the establishment of his regime by casting a new cauldron with the inscription of new constitution. This was an indication for the people that a new regime has taken over. The new emperor used this cauldron to prepare sacrificial offerings to appease the Lord of the Heavens, and also to inculcate virtue and goodness among the subjects.

Opinion

This hexagram should be read in continuity with the previous one, i.e. 49. The 6th strong line shows cauldron with rings of jade. Whenever a new regime takes over it promulgates its own laws and acts for the people to follow. This ancient practice of change in establishing a new order still persists. It should not be forgotten that the new emperor must encourage the men of intrinsic worth and merit in order to become popular among the people. Change should aim at the amelioration of the lot of the people.

51. THE FIFTY- FIRST HEXAGRAM (Taking Action or Moving, Exciting Power)

Here we find the Yang at the initial stage, where the action commences at the bottom and moves towards the topmost position. We, also notice two firm and strong Yang elements at the initial spot and at the 4th place. Trigrams refer to 'Thunder' and also the 'eldest son'.

Opinion

The chief characteristic of the trigram is moving power. It throws broad hints that the society is no longer stagnant, but is in a state of motion. The conduct of the 'superior man' in such a situation of turmoil has to be watched carefully. He must tread cautiously and be fully apprised of the dangers lurking ahead or waiting in the wings. He may surmount all those problems and conquer the divisive forces in the society through smiles, cheerfulness. Like a sincere devotee he will not feel scared. Initial apprehension will ultimately give way to cheerfulness and victory over the forces of revolution and rebellions. This is why this Hexagram means 'taking action or moving or advancing upwards' and gives the impression of 'ease and development'.

52. THE FIFTY- SECOND HEXAGRAM (Resting or Keeping Motionless and Still)

Here the hexagram consists of two trigrams – both referring to one mountain resting over the other. The mountains rise majestically with all their grandeur and curve, as if kissing the sky but firmly planted and entrenched in the soil of the earth. Thus they reveal two-fold characteristic of theirs – both active and passive and resting and arresting. But resting or keeping still can be the right interpretation. The symbols used here are those of toes and calves at rest (1st two Yin lines, then the 3rd strong. Yang line refers to the 'loins' at rest, but the subject is full of excitement at heart. Then his body and cheek bones are kept at rest (two weak Yin) and finally he maintains his complete restfulness and reveals his generosity and magnanimity.

Opinion

It is the 6th firm and strong Yang element that reveals the majestic height and resting posture of a mountain. It closely means that the subject will devotedly emulate the majesty and resting posture of the mountain to the advantage of all. It is like fully resting on one's back and in his slumber one becomes oblivious of himself and surroundings. In that state of complete loss of self consciousness, when he walks in his compound and sees none there, there will of course be no error, i.e. there will be good smiling back upon him. Thus, in this hexagram we find two strong and firm Yang symbols, i.e. the one at the 3rd place and the other at the 6th place. The 3rd one represents motion and the 6th one refers to complete rest. Naturally this hexagram reports both action and rest or motion and stillness.

53. THE FIFTY- THIRD HEXAGRAM (Advancing or Progressing Slowly)

This hexagram refers to gradual progress or advancement. The symbol is that of water which flows gradually and steadily. It also symbolises the progress of the officers to position of authority but such a promotion must take place steadily and methodically.

Opinion

Let us refer to the analogy of a maiden being married to an eligible bachelor. The weak Yin at the 2nd spot refers to the bride and the firm Yang at the 5th place represents respective bridegroom. The process must gradually develop. Thus the hexagram tells us of the marriage of a young maiden. Such a marriage will usher in a period of good fortune and will be advantageous for both the parties.

54. THE FIFTY- FOURTH HEXAGRAM (The Marrying Lady or Marrying Away of a Daughter)

Literal meaning of this hexagram is 'the marrying away of a daughter', but the better interpretation is the marrying lady. In other words, the marriage in this case is initiated by the maiden and her friends. She straightaway goes to her husband's house. It is against all propriety and customs ordained by the Heaven. It is the bridegroom who goes to the bride's house to fetch her with great aplomb. But here, there is the complete reversal of roles; hence most inauspicious.

Opinion

The weak Yin at the 3rd and 5th places represents the maiden and surprisingly both the weak and yielding elements are mounted on the firm Yang.

Such a placement is not in order as both the parties are mismatched; the lady is aggressive and the husband is docile. There is also a great difference of ages between the couples. Such marriages should be rejected outrightly. Hence misfortune awaits such couple.

55. THE FIFTY- FIFTH HEXAGRAM (Abundant Prosperity)

This hexagram teaches the king as to how he should maintain the abundance of prosperity and not to allow it to slide downwards. When the graph of prosperity touches all-time high point, it then starts going downhill. The intelligent and wise ruler will be able to preserve the prosperity and wealth of the state and the people through sheer force of character. Let him be the chief motivating force.

Opinion

We find the yielding Yin at the 5th place. It is, of course, the central and supreme place. The king should not show any anxiety in this context and must attach great value to abundance of prosperity. He should be like the sun at noon–brilliant and at its brightest. Let all be bedazzled with his effulgence.

He should be the chief motivating force and should enlighten all with his bright radiance. In short when the country has reached the climax of prosperity, the king should act as the friend, philosopher and guide like the sun at noon.

56. THE FIFTY- SIXTH HEXAGRAM (Traveling Abroad)

The ancient Chinese were fond of travelling abroad in search of new adventures and also to transact business with the visiting country. This Hexagram teaches all such Chinese travellers to imbibe the lessons of humility and integrity. Their correct behaviour and courteous manners will be the protecting shields for them in alien lands. This way not only they escape harm to their bodies and money, but also win the confidence of the people: This will fill their wallet with lot of money.

Opinion

Such travellers are the ambassadors of goodwill. They by virtue of their good behaviour and impeccable credentials, bring a good name to their country. They also boost their own trade.

57. THE FIFTY- SEVENTH HEXAGRAM

(Flexibility and Penetration or Moving Humbly)

This hexagram is the symbol of both wind and wood and its chief characteristics are flexibility or docility and penetration. Wind can penetrate into every nook and corner; hence it has power of penetration. Water represents flexibility as it proceeds humbly onwards. According to Confucius, relationship between the high and low should be that of wind and grass. The grass must bow and kneel when the wind blows over it. Obviously it refers to the domination of the government over the people.

Opinion

There are two weak Yin lines – one at the bottom of the lower trigram and the other at the bottom of the upper trigram. In order to get joy and advantage, one must proceed humbly. Humility and flexibility in one's attitude is not a weakness but it is a sign of greatness. The greater the man the more humble or mild-mannered he is! This hexagram says that there will be some little attainment and progress, and there will be advantage in movement in whatsoever direction one proceeds. Meeting with the great man will mean better results.

58. THE FIFTY- EIGHTH HEXAGRAM (Pleasure or Joy)

The subject of this Hexagram is pleasure or contentment. The firm Yang elements at the 2nd and 5th spots are correctly placed and they obey the laws ordained by the Heaven. It should be read in continuity with the previous hexagram, i.e. no.57. Humility is the precursor of pleasure; where there is humbleness there is pleasure and joy too.

Opinion

This hexagram tells us that there will be progress and achievement provided there is firmness in the subject. Firmness will be advantageous. This is what the Heaven desires and the people wish. Humility and pleasure go hand in hand and promote harmony among all.

59. THE FIFTY- NINTH HEXAGRAM (State of Dissipation or Dispersion):

This hexagram is another name for dissipation. It connotes complete alienation from right and wrong. In such a state of mind, the person is unable to distinguish between right or wrong. His mind is oblivious of his environments and there is complete anarchy or disorder in the state. Remedial measures must be taken.

Opinion

The firm Yang is at the 5th place and the yielding Yin is at the 4th place. There will be progress, good fortune and success. The king visits his ancestral temple and is in communion with the Lord of Heaven. It will be advantageous to cross the rivulet, provided there is firmness on his part. The king is the only authority who can redeem the situation–howsoever perilous and re-establish order and peace in the country. His minister who concurs with him will be helpful.

60. THE SIXTIETH HEXAGRAM (Regulating or Restraining or Restricting)

The idea of restricting behind this hexagram refers to Chinese wisdom that even a grain of rice has to be earned through hard work. Regulation of one's expenses makes the nation prosperous. There is a nursery rhyme which teaches us the lesson of frugality and restricting:

"Little drops of water; little grains of sand,

Make the mighty ocean and the pleasant land".

The Bible also teaches the lesson of hard work:

"In the sweat of thy face, shalt thou eat bread".

Opinion

This hexagram literally refers to the bamboo joints or the joints of human body. It teaches us regulation and restraint. The regulations howsoever severe and difficult can never be permanent; hence there will be progress and success after those difficulties are surmounted. Overcome the dangers with cheerfulness and andcarryout regulations in their proper positions. The firm Yang at 5th place tells us that only a person of supreme wisdom occupying an eminent position can lead the state to success and prosperity.

61. THE SIXTY- FIRST HEXAGRAM (Inner Most Sincerity)

The message this hexagram propagates is that of innermost sincerity. Sincerity, according to the ancient magic wise men, is the fundamental source of all goodness and virtues. It is the only abiding principle that ushers in harmony in human relationships. It is sincerity in one's relations with other human beings that pays in the long run.

Opinion

One must be sincere from the core of his heart. It is the highest virtue in man and endears him to all – both high and low. Here we find firm Yang lines at the 2nd and 5th places. Sincerity should not be artificial, but should emanate from the deepest recesses of the heart. Only then will it vibrate the chords of others' heart as well.

"Kung Fç" moves even pigs and fish and leads to good fortune. There will, of course, be advantage in crossing the streams provided one is firm and correct".

62. THE SIXTY- SECOND HEXAGRAM (Little Exceeding or Exceeding in What is Small)

Here is a note of warning to all – "Never overdo things". Remain within limits or as Hindus call – "Do not cross Lakshman Rekha"; adopt the path of least resistance, i.e. the middle path. Don't neglect the substance for a minor gain. Things should be done humbly in small matters.

Opinion

Here we have the symbol of a bird. It must remain near the nest where it can perch and relax; it must not soar very high in the regions where there is none to rescue it. In other words one must remain within certain limits. He can exceed the limit a little, i.e. small exceeding. Simply, he may take one step or two beyond the limits prescribed. It is rightly said, "A thousand mile journey is completed by taking a step or two further".

Here we have the yielding Yin at the 2nd and the 5th spots. It means there is fortune ahead in dealing with little affairs, i.e. great affairs should be avoided as far as possible. This will usher in good luck and success.

63. THE SIXTY- THIRD HEXAGRAM (Completed or Being Fulfilled)

This and the next hexagram signifying "completed" and 'not yet accomplished' concluded the great Chinese classic –I Ching. The present hexagram refers to 'successful accomplishment' of the mission and after perfection or complete fulfillment, comes disorder and anarchy. Simply, it means – good fortune in beginning and disorder at the end.

Opinion: The yielding and weak Yin is at the 2nd spot. Everything has been fulfilled and the new government has been consolidated. But while completing the process, the frailty of the human nature must be taken note of. It means there may be disorder after fulfillment or there has been good fortune in the beginning but there is likelihood of anarchy and disorder in the end.

64. THE SIXTY- FOURTH HEXAGRAM (Not Yet Accomplished or Fulfilled)

This hexagram refers to the task 'not yet fulfilled'. Perfection means stagnation and stagnation means death. Society is always in a flux; it never ends. After chaos, there is reconstruction, so is the case with the society. It dies like the legendary phoenix; it gets resurrected from its own ashes. In simple words it means that after fulfillment, there is again the urge to restart the process. The end is just transitory and after a brief lull, again starts the process of beginning.

When the reign of order collapses and anarchy is rampant, do not lose heart, and restart rebuilding the whole superstructure of government and the society again.

The 'I-ching' begins with *'Qian',* i.e. The Heaven, the creative, the strong, the virile, the father and the initiating. The *'Kun',* i.e. The Earth, the receptive, the yielding and the devoted. These two are the symbols of moral conduct. The great book ends with 'Already fulfilled' and 'Not yet fulfilled'. The cycle of life does not cease at all; when it reaches the stage of consummation or perfection it collapses but then a new beginning is made and process of evolution continues till eternity.

Points to Remember

I. Representative Symbols and their Characteristics:

S.No.	Gua	Symbol	Characteristics
1.	Qian (or Chien); {Heaven}	→ ☰	Heaven, initiating, active, firm, strong, virile, father
2.	Kun {Earth}	→ ☷	Earth mother, responding, yielding, devoted, receptive
3.	Zhen (or Chen) {Thunder}	→ ☳	Thunder, arousing, moving, approaching, rising, 1st son
4.	Kan {water}	→ ☵	Water, abysmal, sinking, dangerous, moisturising, below, 2nd son
5.	Ken (or Gen) {Mountain}	→ ☶	Mountain, keeping still, resting, 3rd son, halting, accomplishing
6.	Sun (or Xun) {wind}	→ ☴	Wind, the gentle, penetrating, wood, 1st daughter, assembling, dispersing, lying
7.	Li {Fire}	→ ☲	Fire, clinging, light giving, 2nd daughter, illuminating, radiating
8.	Tui (or Dui) {Lake}	→ ☱	Lake, the joyous, joyful, 3rd daughter, delighting, determining, pleasing, seeing

(‘Gua’ means “hanging up” the symbols for everyone to behold)

II. ‘Yang’

The firm unbroken line signifies the male, positive and active principle. The undivided line is called ‘strong’. All such lines are also called ‘Nine’.

III. ‘Yin’

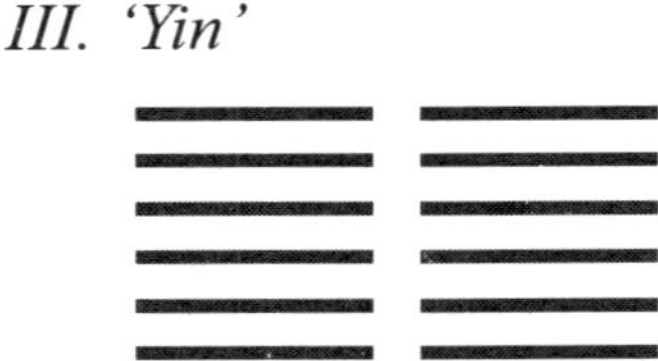

The weak broken line signifies the female negative and passive principle. The divided line is called ‘weak’. All such divided lines are also called ‘sex’.

IV. Each hexagram consists of two Trigrams; the lower one called ‘The Inner’ and the one above is called ‘The Outer’.

'I-ching' is one of the greatest treatises on oriental philosophy. It should be read not just as a book on 'divination' or 'fortune telling' but also as a 'Book of wisdom'. It is full of gems and pearls of knowledge and wisdom. In order to get these precious gems, the reader must dive deep or dig deep; then he will become wiser and a better human being. It is an unfathomable ocean; the more we explore, the more remains to be explored. As regards its fortune telling system, the answers are not precise. Sometimes they appear ambiguous to a layman, but only an expert of 'I-Ching' can give exact interpretation. It requires a lot of devotion, dedication, toil and study.